Checklist for Life
for Men

Checklist for Life
for Men

THOMAS NELSON PUBLISHERS®
Nashville

A Division of Thomas Nelson, Inc.
www.ThomasNelson.com

Published in Nashville, Tennessee, by Thomas Nelson, Inc.

Managing Editor: Lila Empson
Manuscript written by Todd Hafer, Mark Moesta, Mark Weising, and Kyle Olund in conjunction with Snapdragon Editorial Group, Inc.
Design: Whisner Design Group

Checklist for life for men.
    p. cm.
ISBN 0-7852-6463-9 (pbk.)
1. Men–Religious life. I. Thomas Nelson Publishers.
BV4440 .C45 2002
248.8'42—dc21
                              2002005956

Printed in the United States of America

        02 03 04 05 06   CJK   5 4 3 2

Heart Attitude

I will trust God in all things.

Table of Contents

Table of Contents Continued

Introduction

I will welcome you and be your Father. You will be my sons and my daughters, as surely as I am God.

—2 CORINTHIANS 6:17–18 CEV

A man's life is filled with friendly chaos—work, relationships, health, spirituality, and that's just the beginning. So how does a guy hope to stay afloat, make a difference, in the midst of it all? That's a tall order.

Checklist for Life for Men was designed to bring that friendly chaos into focus, to help you achieve balance, avoid extremity, create a degree of order in your day-to-day living.

This is not a feel-good book filled with warm-and-fuzzy inspiration. It's a call-to-action book that will point the way to a better, more productive, more satisfying, more contentment-filled daily lifestyle. As you read, consider the principles communicated in the overview or insight passages and decide to do each checklist to help make those principles active in your life. The I Will checklists comprise heart attitudes that will help put you in the right frame of mind. The Things to Do checklists will help put hands and feet to your heart attitudes and show how to translate them into straightforward action.

In Things to Remember, abundant scriptures give sound, biblical support to each insight passage. "To know wisdom and instruction, to perceive the words of understanding, to receive the instruction of wisdom, justice, judgment, and equity; to give prudence to the simple, to the young man knowledge and discretion—a wise man will hear and increase learning and a man of understanding will attain wise counsel" (Proverbs 1:2–5).

There are also topical quotations to inspire and motivate you. Consider this by Tryon Edwards: "He who never changes his opinions, never corrects his mistakes, will never be wiser on the morrow than he is today."

It is our hope that this book will play a part in your journey of awareness and betterment. It is also our prayer that the principles affirmed in these insights will be established in your life and passed along to others.

A man's lot is not an easy one. But it is one made easier by wisdom and with the help of God. As you read, open your heart and mind to what God is saying to you about every aspect of your life, and invite God's Spirit to be with you on your journey.

No man ever wanted anything so much as God wants to make the soul aware of him.
—MEISTER ECKHART

God demonstrates His own love toward us, in that while we were still sinners, Christ died for us.

ROMANS 5:8 NKJV

What lies behind us and what lies before us are small matters compared to what lies within us.

RALPH WALDO EMERSON

Come unto me, all ye that labour and are heavy laden, and I will give you rest.

MATTHEW 11:28 KJV

By his first work God gave me to myself; and by the next he gave himself to me. And when he gave himself, he gave me back myself that I had lost.

BERNARD OF CLAIRVAUX

When you search for me, you will find me; if you seek me with all your heart. I will let you find me, says the LORD.

JEREMIAH 29:13–14 NRSV

Two men please God—who serves him with all his heart because he knows him; who seeks him with all his heart because he knows him not.

NIKITA IVANOVICH PANIN

When God says to your disturbed, distracted, restless soul or mind, "Come unto me," he is saying, come out of the strife and doubt and struggle of what is at the moment where you stand, into that which was and is and is to be—the eternal, the essential, the absolute.
—PHILLIPS BROOKS

Checklist for Life *for* Men

God is to us like the sky to a small bird, which cannot see its outer limits and cannot reach its distant horizons, but can only lose itself in the greatness and immensity of the blueness.

—John Powell

Can you fathom the mysteries of God? Can you probe the limits of the Almighty? They are higher than the heavens—what can you do? Their measure is longer than the earth and wider than the sea.

—Job 11:7–9 NIV

Peace

The Gift that Keeps On Giving

The LORD gives strength to his people; the LORD blesses his people with peace.

—PSALM 29:11 NCV

Jesus is called the "Prince of Peace" in the Bible, which tells a lot about how His followers are to live. God doesn't want you to be stressed out or full of worry. He wants you to live in freedom from all that tries to hold you down. That's tough if you think it is a sign of weakness to be at peace with yourself. If you can't fret and get worked up about things, what else is there for you to do?

Does living a peace-filled life mean that God will arrange your life in such a way that you'll face no uncertainties and have clear sailing through life? No. In fact, life may be harder for a follower (remember Job?), but God will equip you with a supernatural peace to help keep your focus on Him no matter what. A lot of men throughout history—strong men—lived with peace in their hearts and trusted God in all circumstances.

The shepherd boy David had every right to be nervous when he confronted Goliath, considering David's size, the giant's stature, and the fear among the great warriors of his people's army. But God brought a peace over him and gave him confidence that he could defeat the enemy. Do you have a Goliath threatening you? Ask God to give your heart the same kind of peace.

God pared down Gideon's army from ten thousand to three hundred before He sent them off to fight. Surely Gideon had good reason to get bent out of shape and to worry. Yet God gave him peace about the situation so that he could trust God rather than himself or his men. Are you relying too much on everything and everyone but Him?

To bring the idea of God's peace closer to home, talk to someone who lived through the Great Depression or fought in World War II. That generation, though faced with seeming insurmountable odds, remained calm through their trying circumstances and trusted largely upon an unwavering faith in God.

God does not grant peace to only a select few. He offers it to all who would believe in Him. The next time you are in a situation where the weight of the world seems to be on your shoulders, stop and turn your attention to the God who promises to give you a peace that passes all understanding.

I Will

Trust God in all things.

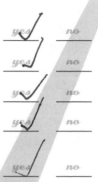

yes ✓   no

Believe that everything works out for the good.

yes ✓   no

Attempt to bring to mind matters that are
stressing me out so I can offer them to
God for Him to take away.

yes ✓   no

Take comfort in God's promises of peace to me.

yes ✓   no

Accept peace as a gift from God.

yes ✓   no

Allow God's peace to rule in my heart.

yes ✓   no

Be conscious of how others around me live in
peace.

yes ✓   no

Things to Do

☐ *Make a list of things keeping me from a peace-filled life.*

☐ *Write down all of God's blessings He has given you and the promises He has kept.*

☐ *One by one, ask God to give you peace where it is missing, and thank Him for where it exists.*

☐ *Seek out someone older than you (preferably much older) who lives a peace-filled life.*

☐ *Tell this person what is keeping your heart from peace, and ask for some advice.*

☐ *Ask God to take away all your worries and fears and to fill you with peace—abundant peace.*

Things to Remember

Great peace have those who love Your law, and nothing causes them to stumble.

PSALM 119:165 NKJV

Acquaint yourself with Him, and be at peace; thereby good will come to you.

JOB 22:21 NKJV

Jesus said, "Peace I leave with you, My peace I give to you; not as the world gives do I give to you. Let not your heart be troubled, neither let it be afraid."

JOHN 14:27 NKJV

Let the peace of God rule in your hearts, to which also you were called in one body; and be thankful.

COLOSSIANS 3:15 NKJV

The peace of God, which surpasses all understanding, will guard your hearts and minds through Christ Jesus.

PHILIPPIANS 4:7 NKJV

Grace to you and peace from God our Father and the Lord Jesus Christ.

2 CORINTHIANS 1:2 NKJV

Scatter the clouds that hide

The face of heaven, and show

Where sweet peace doth abide,

Where Truth and Beauty grow.

—ROBERT SEYMOUR BRIDGES

Joy is like restless day; but peace divine

Like quiet night;

Lead me, O Lord,— till perfect Day shall shine

Through Peace to Light.

—ADELAIDE ANNE PROCTER

Go Boldly Where No Man Has Gone Before

Do not throw away this confident trust in the Lord, no matter what happens. Remember the great reward it brings you!

—HEBREWS 10:35 NLT

Men were created to live dangerous, adventurous lives, to live boldly in everything they do. You know this because you know that God created you in His image, and He is all powerful. In fact the Bible says that "Warrior" is His name.

Does that mean that you can do and say whatever you want and say to others, "If you don't like it, tough"? God does not want you to be a bully—even a spiritual bully. Jesus, when He was on earth, was tough when He had to be; he didn't back down from anyone. He was no wimp, but He also did not go around intimidating others or bossing them around. He was loving and caring, and he lived from a servant's heart.

The degrees that you may earn, the number of years that you may attain in your career, and the higher tax bracket that you may reach are all good signs in your life, but true confidence is inherited. True confidence comes from the spiritual genes passed on to you by your heavenly Father. Living boldly is nothing more than knowing who you are as a child of God and understanding how He wants to use you.

If you're a salesman, sell boldly! Don't approach a potential deal with doubt in your mind. Talk with the person, as if you expect the transaction to happen. If you have to give a presentation at a meeting, present boldly! Prepare more than you need to, stand tall and straight in front of your audience, and speak clearly and with authority, conviction, and passion. Whatever you do, wherever you go, act like the ambassador of almighty God that you are.

What about when you don't feel all that bold? Circumstances may come your way where you feel that you don't have what it takes—that maybe you should just step aside and wait until things get easier. Don't listen to that lie! Open your Bible and read some of the apostle Paul's letters. He was faced with all kinds of oppositions and threats against his life, yet he did not back down. And when you think you cannot go it alone, turn to your fellow brothers in Christ and go into battle together.

Thank God for filling you with His strength and confidence, which He gives to you abundantly if you seek to live your life as a reflection of Him.

I Will

See myself as a godly warrior and not as a religious wimp.

yes ✓   no

Believe that I was created in the image of the almighty God.

yes ✓   no

Recognize God as the source of my strength.

yes ✓   no

Approach each day looking for opportunities to win rather than looking for ways to simply survive.

yes ✓   no

Align myself with other men who are living courageous lives for God.

yes ✓   no

Keep hope at the front of my mind at all times, expecting to be victorious through God's strength.

yes ✓   no

Things to Do

☐ *Make a list of all of your strengths.*

☐ *On the same sheet of paper, write down your weaknesses, greatest to smallest.*

☐ *Cross out the weaknesses over which you have no control or those insignificant to your pursuit of spiritual valor, and circle the weaknesses that you know you could transform into strengths.*

☐ *Count up the number of current or projected strengths and compare that number to those you crossed out.*

☐ *Take your smallest weakness and pray about it—ask God to give you opportunities to work on it and the strength to face it head-on.*

☐ *Talk to a close friend or two and ask them to be your allies in your battle to live life boldly in this one area.*

Things to Remember

The Lord is my strength and song, and He has become my salvation.

PSALM 118:14 NKJV

He is my God, and I will praise Him; my father's God, and I will exalt Him.

EXODUS 15:2 NKJV

You, Lord, have made me glad through Your work; I will triumph in the works of Your hands.

PSALM 92:4 NKJV

I saw God before me for all time. Nothing can shake me; he's right by my side. I'm glad from the inside out, ecstatic; I've pitched my tent in the land of hope.

ACTS 2:26 THE MESSAGE

I will not be afraid of ten thousands of people who have set themselves against me all around.

PSALM 3:6 NKJV

God has not given us a spirit of fear, but of power and of love and of a sound mind.

2 TIMOTHY 1:7 NKJV

You have confidence in yourself, which is valuable, if not an indispensable quality.

—ABRAHAM LINCOLN

I place no hope in my strength, nor in my works: but all my confidence is in God my protector, who never abandons those who have put all their hope and thought in him.

—FRANÇOIS RABELAIS

Wisdom

A Real Wise Guy

You desire honesty from the heart, so you can teach me to be wise in my inmost being.

—Psalm 51:6 NLT

How many smart people do you know? You might be able to fill up an entire page of names—instructors, bosses, colleagues, accountants, doctors, scientists, librarians, businessmen, attorneys, financial consultants . . . the list goes on.

Now think about how many wise people you know. If you need more than one hand on which to count them, you are truly blessed. There is no shortage of intelligence, education, and training, so why does wisdom seem to be in such short supply? God calls you to seek out wisdom—to seek the company of those who possess it and to be wise yourself.

Just looking in one translation of the Bible, the New King James Version, you'll find the word *wise* in 197 different verses and the word *wisdom* in 215. As for the words *smart* and *intelligent*, you'll find them in only 0 and 1 verse, respectively. What's the difference? Being smart is knowing about something, whereas being wise is discerning what to do with that knowledge. An extreme example that illustrates this point: Being smart is knowing how to build a bomb; being wise is knowing what to do—or not to do—with that bomb.

A smart doctor is someone who has had the best education and is up-to-date on new technology and medical research. A wise doctor, though, is discerning in difficult situations, and he makes timely decisions that are correct. A smart pastor has graduated from a seminary and can cite thousands of facts about the Bible. A wise pastor, on the other hand, can easily take a centuries-old Scripture passage and bring it alive and make it relevant for the twenty-first century. A smart supervisor may have read all the best-selling books on leadership, managerial styles, and budget streamlining, but a wise supervisor understands his staff, knows how and when to motivate individuals, and can easily change direction when necessary.

Wisdom takes time. You cannot say, "Tomorrow I will be wise." Much goes into the making of a wise man.

Though having great intelligence doesn't necessarily make you wise, intellect will definitely assist you in your pursuit of wisdom. Read great literature—classics, history books, biographies, how-to guides, and in-depth Bible study books. Keep a journal of all you are learning, and look for opportunities in your everyday life to apply your newfound knowledge.

Meditating on and obeying God's Word is another way to increase your wisdom. What better place to seek it than in such books of the Bible as Psalms, Proverbs, and the four

Gospels, to begin with. Our God is an all-knowing God, and He loves when you come and seek the wisdom He is waiting to pour out on you. As you read through Scripture, pray that God will reveal to you hidden truths and open doors you never knew existed.

You will also gain a great deal of wisdom by surrounding yourself with wise individuals. Usually these men are older gentlemen who truly know what they are talking about—whenever they open their mouths. Observe how they live their lives and ask them why they make certain decisions. Find out about their past and ask them what they hope the future brings. Seek out their counsel on matters of your heart, and when they offer you guidance, take notes.

One more way you can gain wisdom, which is almost always the last place a person wants to look, is learning from your mistakes. As you experience life, you mess up—again and again. The messing-up part is something each man is all too familiar with but has learned to accept. The hard part is gleaning from those incidents all that you can so you might avoid them in the future. The next time you make a mistake, write the situation down and analyze it. Ask yourself what happened, what you could have done differently, and how you can avoid it or anticipate it in the future. Once you start seeing mistakes as assets and not liabilities, your wisdom will grow deeper.

No one is born with wisdom. People grow into it. And if that is what you want, God will grant you wisdom, maybe even a wisdom like Solomon's.

I Will

Look at wisdom as more valuable than silver
and gold.   _yes_   _no_

Be patient in my pursuit of wisdom.   _yes_   _no_

See my mistakes as opportunities to grow.   _yes_   _no_

Seek to understand rather than just to collect
information.   _yes_   _no_

Expect God to bless me with the wisdom that I seek.   _yes_   _no_

Concern myself more with where I want to grow in
wisdom than where other people are.   _yes_   _no_

Things to Do

☐ Read the book of Proverbs.

☐ Write down and put in your wallet the one proverb that most
profoundly speaks to you.

☐ Read that proverb at least five times today and memorize it by the end
of tomorrow.

☐ Think of three areas in your life for which you'd like greater wisdom,
and write down a handful of questions for each—whatever pops into
your head.

☐ Get together with an elder gentleman whom you respect greatly in the
area of wisdom, and give him the list of questions you wrote out.

☐ Listen to him speak and don't say anything unless he asks you
something.

Things to Remember

Happy is the man who finds wisdom, and the man who gains understanding; for her proceeds are better than the profits of silver, and her gain than fine gold.

PROVERBS 3:13–14 NKJV

The Lord GOD has given Me the tongue of the learned, that I should know how to speak a word in season to him who is weary. He awakens Me morning by morning, he awakens My ear to hear as the learned.

ISAIAH 50:4 NKJV

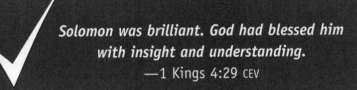

Solomon was brilliant. God had blessed him with insight and understanding.
—1 Kings 4:29 CEV

The spirit of the LORD shall rest upon him, the spirit of wisdom and understanding, the spirit of counsel and might, the spirit of knowledge and of the fear of the LORD.

ISAIAH 11:2 KJV

Buy the truth, and do not sell it, also wisdom and instruction and understanding.

PROVERBS 23:23 NKJV

By pride comes nothing but strife, but with the well-advised is wisdom.

PROVERBS 13:10 NKJV

Give me wisdom and knowledge, that I may go out and come in before this people; for who can judge this great people of Yours?

2 CHRONICLES 1:10 NKJV

If any of you lacks wisdom, let him ask of God, who gives to all liberally and without reproach, and it will be given to him.

JAMES 1:5 NKJV

How can men be wise? The only way to begin is by reverence for God. For growth in wisdom comes from obeying his laws. Praise his name forever.

PSALM 111:10 TLB

Teach us to number our days, that we may gain a heart of wisdom.

PSALM 90:12 NKJV

I pray for you constantly, asking God, the glorious Father of our Lord Jesus Christ, to give you wisdom to see clearly and really understand who Christ is and all that he has done for you.

EPHESIANS 1:16–17 NKJV

Wisdom cannot prevent a fall, but may cushion it.
—MASON COOLEY

And wisdom is a butterfly
And not a gloomy bird of prey.
—WILLIAM BUTLER YEATS

Commitment

Seeing Things Through

Jesus said, "He who endures to the end shall be saved."
—MATTHEW 24:13 NKJV

Watch a televised marathon, and you'll see an interesting phenomenon. As the starter gun fires, a few novice runners will sprint to the front of the pack. Those attention-grabbers will enjoy a few moments on camera, but it is unlikely that they will cross the finish line twenty-six-plus miles later. Finishing a marathon requires patience, perspective, endurance, strength, and just plain grit. It's a lot like life.

You can bring a champion marathoner's commitment to your life's goals—ensuring that you will start fresh and finish strong—by following the three *P*'s: preparation, perspective, and perseverance.

Preparation. The early breakout sprinters from the first paragraph couldn't finish the race they started so briskly because they weren't prepared for the long challenge ahead of them. Perhaps they didn't train well or formulate a race plan to ensure they were mentally ready.

Don't make that mistake. Prepare yourself to achieve

your goals. For example, if you want to lose fifteen pounds, prepare yourself by reading what qualified people have to say about the subject. Talk with family members or friends who have been successful shedding weight and keeping it off. Enlist their support.

Perspective. A marathoner realizes that he has a long race before him. He doesn't get caught up in the early excitement and expend too much energy at the beginning. He paces himself.

You can do the same thing. For example, if you decide to get an advanced degree, pace yourself. Don't take too many classes up-front. And don't try to read all your text materials in the first month.

Perspective can also help you at the middle or near the end of your endeavor. When a marathoner hits the midpoint of his race, he can tell himself, *I don't even have to run a marathon any more—only a half-marathon!*

Perseverance. Any goal will present obstacles and disappointments. Even with all the preparation and perspective in the world, you may reach a point of mental and physical fatigue as you strive to finish what you've started.

Times like these require perseverance. Willpower. Determination. Grit. Remind yourself what your goal is, how much it means to you, and how you will feel if you don't achieve it.

You might not have the stamina of an elite marathon runner, but you can match his or her determination. And when you finish what you've begun, you can share in the triumph.

I Will

Stay focused on, and committed to, my key life goals.

yes _no_

Be patient as I strive to achieve my goals.

yes _no_

Avoid letting fatigue, self-doubt, or criticism from others trip me up as strive to fulfill ambitions.

yes _no_

Share my goals with God and ask Him for the wisdom and the will to achieve them.

yes _no_

Build and maintain strong relationships with people who can help me achieve my goals.

yes _no_

Always note the progress I have made toward accomplishing what I set out to do.

yes _no_

Things to Do

☐ _Write down a major life goal and a timetable for achieving it._

☐ _Share your goal with a friend or family member and ask him or her to help keep you accountable._

☐ _Celebrate with this person every time you make a significant step toward your goal._

☐ _Read an article by or about someone who has achieved a goal similar to yours._

☐ _Read the first chapter of James to get God's perspective on perseverance and commitment._

☐ _Make a list of possible obstacles along the pathway toward your goal and devise a plan for overcoming or eliminating them._

Things to Remember

May the God of all grace, who called us to His eternal glory by Christ Jesus, after you have suffered a while, perfect, establish, strengthen, and settle you.

1 PETER 5:10 NKJV

Our light affliction, which is but for a moment, is working for us a far more exceeding and eternal weight of glory.

2 CORINTHIANS 4:17 NKJV

Jesus said, "Which of you, intending to build a tower, does not sit down first and count the cost, whether he has enough to finish it."

LUKE 14:28 NKJV

The Lord GOD will help Me; therefore I will not be disgraced; therefore I have set My face like a flint, and I know that I will not be ashamed.

ISAIAH 50:7 NKJV

Be strong and do not let your hands be weak, for your work shall be rewarded!

2 CHRONICLES 15:7 NKJV

He will give eternal life to everyone who has patiently done what is good in the hope of receiving glory, honor, and life that lasts forever.

ROMANS 2:7 CEV

The person who makes a success of living is the one who sees his goal steadily and aims for it unswervingly. That is dedication.

—CECIL B. DE MILLE

The profundity of a spiritual act is in direct proportion to its author's commitment.

—HENRI DE LUBAC

Companionship

He's Right by Your Side

God is faithful, by whom you were called into the fellowship of His Son, Jesus Christ our Lord.

—1 Corinthians 1:9 NKJV

Who is your all-time best friend? The one person you would single out above all the others? Think for a few moments about what makes this friend shine brighter than the others.

Do you and your best friend share some common interests? What things do you admire about him—a sense of humor, intelligence, confidence, generosity? When you are together, do you find that your personalities complement one another?

These are important factors, but they probably don't get to the core of what gives your best friend the number-one position in your heart and mind. Think about it—isn't your best friend the one you trust more than the others? The one you can depend on to be by your side, regardless of circumstances or consequences? The one with whom you can share secret fears or go to for advice on sensitive— even embarrassing—matters?

Jesus is that kind of companion. You may have

thought of Him as your leader, your teacher, and the Lord of your life. And He is all of those things. But Jesus is also your friend. In the New Testament, Jesus reveals that those who follow Him are His friends, not just disciples or devotees.

Acknowledging Jesus as your friend can bring a whole new dynamic to your relationship with Him.

Realizing that Jesus is your friend can make your relationship with Him closer. The role of teacher-student or employer-employee can be a barrier to closeness. In fact, many teachers and managers are cautioned to avoid becoming too close to those under their authority.

But it's a different story with friends. Since Jesus calls you a friend, there is no professionally mandated distance between the two of you. You can get as close as you want. You can dispense with the formalities and pour out your heart to Him. You can be honest with Him. You can cry before Him if you need to. And, as with any true friend, His door is always open.

Because Jesus is your friend, you can communicate with Him about anything. Jesus will listen to your thoughts, opinions, and concerns, regardless of the topic. You can go to Him even when you aren't seeking wisdom or guidance. You can approach Jesus merely to tell Him how you feel.

Now review the question in the first paragraph. If God has blessed you with an earthly best friend, you are fortunate indeed. But don't forget that you have a heavenly Best Friend too. And He would love to hear from you.

I Will

Remember always that I have a true friend in Jesus.   *yes*   *no*

Invest time in my friendship with Jesus, just as I should in any relationship that is important to me.   *yes*   *no*

Be open, honest, and respectful toward Jesus, and all of my friends.   *yes*   *no*

Allow God to show me how to be a better friend.   *yes*   *no*

Love others, including my Lord and Savior, unselfishly.   *yes*   *no*

Ask for forgiveness when I wrong a friend.   *yes*   *no*

Make my friendship with Jesus and with others the kind of relationships that others will want to model.   *yes*   *no*

Things to Do

☐ *Read the Old Testament story of David and Jonathan to learn about a model friendship.*

☐ *Write a letter, prayer, or psalm to Jesus, thanking Him for being such a faithful friend.*

☐ *The next time you face a personal crisis or challenge, turn to Jesus first.*

☐ *Memorize Proverbs 17:17—"A friend loves at all times."*

☐ *Create a list of ten things to do to build a deeper friendship with Jesus.*

☐ *Thank God for providing His Son, not only as our Savior, but also as our friend.*

Things to Remember

Jesus said, "Behold, I stand at the door and knock. If anyone hears My voice and opens the door, I will come in to him and dine with him, and he with Me."

REVELATION 3:20 NKJV

Jesus said, "You are My friends if you do whatever I command you."

JOHN 15:14 NKJV

I will be a Father to you, and you shall be My sons and daughters, says the Lord Almighty.

2 CORINTHIANS 6:18 NKJV

I am continually with You; You hold me by my right hand.

PSALM 73:23 NKJV

Blessed are those who dwell in Your house; they will still be praising You.

PSALM 84:2 NKJV

The LORD is near to all who call upon Him, to all who call upon Him in truth.

PSALM 145:18 NKJV

The relationship between God and a man is more private and intimate than any possible relation between two fellow creatures.

—C. S. LEWIS

God desires and is pleased to communicate with us through the avenues of our minds, our wills, and our emotions. The continuous and unembarrassed interchange of love and thought between God and the souls of the redeemed men and women is the throbbing heart of the New Testament.

—A. W. TOZER

Children

Point Your Children in the Right Direction

Fathers, do not provoke your children to wrath: but bring them up in the training and admonition of the Lord.

—EPHESIANS 6:4 NKJV

Walking through a heavily wooded national park, a man saw a large tree that was growing crooked. Near the tree, someone had placed a straight, stout pole and tied it to the tree with ropes—in an effort to help straighten it. Unfortunately, the upper part of the tree had grown out so far from its trunk that there was no way to correct the misdirected growth. The crooked part of the tree was simply too far from the corrective pole.

The same thing can happen to parents. Thinking they are doing the right thing, some parents let their children run wild during their early days—not wanting to correct them and risk being thought of as mean or overly strict. They fear alienating their kids, or breaking their spirits.

But, before long, these parents find they can't control their wayward children, especially as they reach adolescence. Often, the now-frantic parents turn to a therapist or a school counselor for help, but those outside sources find it difficult to undo the damage of years of overly permissive, directionless parenting.

Children need consistent direction and, occasionally, correction when they have violated parental rules or made a poor decision. Such leadership creates clear expectations and shows kids that someone cares enough about them to steer their lives toward the right path.

In Proverbs 22:6, the Bible encourages parents to "train up a child in the way he should go, and when he is old, he will not depart from it." The word used for *train* in this verse is the same one applied to Hebrew midwives' ancient practice of putting a bit of tasty juice on their fingers to help newborn babies learn how to nurse.

To train, in this sense, means to create an appetite for doing the right thing, the healthy thing. It means nurturing good habits and behaviors and showing how irresponsible behavior ultimately damages the quality of one's life—not to mention the lives of those who love that person.

Even if you don't have children, you are probably an adult in some child's life. Or you may be a parent through adoption, a blended family, or good, old-fashioned childbirth. In almost every circumstance, you have an exciting opportunity to help someone grow straight, tall, and strong. Use the Bible's principles, the example of good parents that you know, and your own wisdom and experience to make your child's (or children's) formative years the foundation for a rewarding, productive, and God-honoring life.

I Will

Realize that children need direction and guidance—even if they don't ask for it.

yes *no*

Avoid letting my desire to be a "cool dad" keep me from applying loving but firm correction when it's needed.

yes *no*

Seek God's wisdom as I strive to be a great dad.

yes *no*

Pray for my children every day.

yes *no*

Love my children deeply and unselfishly.

yes *no*

Be confident and secure enough to admit to my children when I've made a mistake or an unwise decision.

yes *no*

Things to Do

☐ *Within the next year, find an exemplary dad whose parenting you can emulate and whose advice and support you can see.*

☐ *Memorize Ephesians 6:4—"You, fathers, do not provoke your children to wrath: but bring them up in the training and admonition of the Lord."*

☐ *During the next month, come up with—and begin implementing—ten creative ways to have more meaningful times with your children, including times to teach important life principles.*

☐ *Think of a father-child tradition that you can begin on a birthday or other significant day in a child's life. (For example, a camping trip on the first weekend after school ends, or a dinner at a fancy restaurant on a birthday.)*

Things to Remember

Moses said to the Israelites, "You shall therefore keep His statutes and His commandments which I command you today, that it may go well with you and with your children after you, and that you may prolong your days in the land which the LORD your God is giving you for all time."

DEUTERONOMY 4:40 NKJV

The LORD said, "All your children shall be taught by the LORD, and great shall be the peace of your children."

ISAIAH 54:13 NKJV

Correct your son, and he will give you rest; yes, he will give delight to your soul.

PROVERBS 29:17 NKJV

Children, obey your parents in the Lord, for this is right. "Honor your father and mother," which is the first commandment with promise: "that it may be well with you and you may live long on the earth."

EPHESIANS 6:1–3 NKJV

Foolishness is bound up in the heart of a child; the rod of correction will drive it far from him.

PROVERBS 22:15 NKJV

Children are not casual guests in our homes. They have been loaned to us temporarily for the purpose of loving them and instilling a foundation of values on which their future lives will be built.
—JAMES DOBSON

It is common sense to put the seal to the wax while it is soft.
—ARTHUR JACKSON

Daily Walk

Exercising Your Faith

When Abram was ninety-nine years old, the LORD appeared to Abram and said to him, "I am Almighty God; walk before Me and be blameless."

—GENESIS 17:1 NKJV

On a whim, Rob decided to enter a marathon, two weeks before the race date. His friends warned him, "Are you sure you're ready to run 26.2 miles? That's an awfully long race, and you haven't been running much lately." But Rob ignored the warnings. *After all,* he reasoned, *I've completed marathons before, and I'm a natural runner.*

As race day drew near, Rob considered going for a long run to assess his fitness level. But he decided against it, feeling he might tire himself out or get injured. He also thought about modifying his diet, cutting back on sweets, and increasing his intake of energy-providing complex carbohydrates and muscle-building protein. But again he reconsidered. *It's probably too late for that stuff.*

As Rob stood at the start line on race day, he was optimistic. The weather was perfect, and he felt energized by the throng of runners and the chorus of "Rocky" booming over the loudspeakers.

When the starting gun sounded, he took off at a brisk pace. Three miles flew by. Then five. Then seven. The course offered several long hills, but Rob attacked them with gusto. He felt certain that the few early hills would be the only ones on the course.

At mile ten, Rob began to fatigue. But he didn't panic. He was sure he'd get his second wind soon. But that second wind never came. At mile eleven, Rob hit the wall. His body felt completely drained of energy. He could barely pick up his feet. And, he discovered to his dismay, there were still hills left on the course. Long, steep hills. As he got halfway up one incline, he slowed to a walk.

He felt his muscles stiffening. His head pounded. And he felt blisters forming on the bottom of both feet. Discouraged as he hit the twelve-mile mark, Rob decided he would try to walk the rest of the way. But at the race's halfway point, his left leg cramped up. He limped to the side of the road and tried to massage the cramp away. But every time he tried to walk, the pain returned.

When a volunteer EMT asked him if he needed help, Rob nodded sadly. A few minutes later, he accepted a ride back to the starting line, where, after a few minutes of treatment, he was able to hobble to his car.

Few people would attempt a marathon with no preparation, but a surprising number take a Rob-like approach to their spiritual lives. They don't invest time and energy into their faith relationship with God, and they pay the consequences. For example, a crisis occurs and they panic, feeling unsure of how to respond and guilty as they cry out to a God who they know they've ignored for a long time. Or their faith is challenged by a friend or business associate, and they don't know how to defend their beliefs. Or they attempt to teach a principle of faith to others but find themselves unequipped to explain themselves clearly, or to point to positive examples from their own lives.

Your faith is like any other area of your life. It has to be exercised and put into practice regularly in order for it to grow strong and stay strong. A strong faith can carry you through life's daily, routine challenges, and it can sustain you when crisis invades your life.

Just as a marathoner strengthens his body for a race, there are several ways you can exercise your faith to make it strong and vibrant. Here are a few suggestions:

Commit to daily prayer, Bible reading, and other faith-building books. Once-in-a-while training doesn't work for athletics, and it is inadequate in the spiritual realm as well.

Surround yourself with spiritual training partners—people who can encourage you and advise you as you build a strong faith.

Put your faith into practice every day. Don't just learn biblical principles; put them into action. Whenever you hear a sermon, read a Bible passage, or study a Sunday-school lesson, think of one idea or suggestion that you can implement in the coming week. True faith thrives on the opportunity to prove itself in real life.

I Will

Look for creative ways to build my faith and put it into practice.
yes _no_

Follow Christ's example as a man who lived His faith.
yes _no_

Thank God for the gift of faith, and pledge to use that gift.
yes _no_

Avoid anything that will hinder my faith or my ability to strengthen it.
yes _no_

Pray for ways to share my faith with others.
yes _no_

Ask God how to encourage others in their faith.
yes _no_

Things to Do

☐ _Read Hebrews 11 for a biblical perspective on faith._

☐ _Within the next year, find a spiritual mentor whose faith you can emulate._

☐ _Write your own definition of faith; use it as a periodic checkpoint._

☐ _During the next month, come up with—and begin implementing—ten creative ways to live out your faith in everyday life._

☐ _Drop someone a note of encouragement the next time you see him or her applying faith to daily life._

☐ _During the next year, attend a workshop or symposium on faith-building or on practical faith application._

☐ _Read a short biography about a person you admire for the way he or she put faith into action._

Things to Remember

Moses said, "You shall keep the commandments of the LORD your God, to walk in His ways and to fear Him. For the LORD your God is bringing you into a good land, a land of brooks of water, of fountains and springs, that flow out of valleys and hills."

DEUTERONOMY 8:6–7 NKJV

Listen to my teaching, and you will be wise; do not ignore it. Happy are those who listen to me, watching at my door every day, waiting at my open doorway.

PROVERBS 8:33–34 NCV

> *Teach me Your way, O LORD; I will walk in Your truth; unite my heart to fear Your name.*
> —Psalm 86:11 NKJV

Moses said to the Israelites, "You shall walk in all the ways which the LORD your God has commanded you, that you may live and that it may be well with you, and that you may prolong your days in the land which you shall possess."

DEUTERONOMY 5:33 NKJV

Cause me to hear Your lovingkindness in the morning, for in You do I trust; cause me to know the way in which I should walk, for I lift up my soul to You.

PSALM 143:8 NKJV

Blessed are the undefiled in the way,
who walk in the law of the LORD!

Psalm 119:1 NKJV

We walk by faith, not by sight.

2 CORINTHIANS 5:7 NKJV

The LORD said, "Behold the proud, his
soul is not upright in him; but the just
shall live by his faith."

HABAKKUK 2:4 NKJV

Jesus said, "Whoever comes to Me, and
hears My sayings and does them . . . is
like a man building a house, who dug
deep and laid the foundation on the
rock. And when the flood arose, the
stream beat vehemently against that
house, and could not shake it, for it was
founded on the rock."

LUKE 6:47–48 NKJV

Examine yourselves as to whether you
are in the faith. Test yourselves.

2 CORINTHIANS 13:5 NKJV

I have been crucified with Christ; it is no
longer I who live, but Christ lives in me;
and the life which I now live in the flesh
I live by faith in the Son of God, who
loved me and gave Himself for me.

GALATIANS 2:20 NKJV

**The act of faith is
more than a bare
statement of
belief, it is a
turning to the face
of the living God.**

—CHRISTOPHER BRYANT

**It is cynicism and
fear that freeze
life; it is faith that
thaws it out,
releases it, sets it
free.**

—HARRY EMERSON
FOSDICK

Compassion

Do unto Others

Give, and it will be given to you. . . . For with the same measure that you use, it will be measured back to you.

—LUKE 6:38 NKJV

Perhaps the Golden Rule isn't what it used to be. Bumper stickers proclaim permutations like "Do unto others before they do unto you" or "Do unto others—then split." Motivational speakers talk about *Winning Through Intimidation,* and business leaders and professional sports coaches read books like *The Art of War* for inspiration and guidance.

To some people, the Golden Rule has outlived its usefulness. Or perhaps it seems to them that it applies only to being kind, loving, and compassionate toward the people who show those characteristics in return—or to those who can help them achieve personal or professional goals.

The Bible urges you to treat everyone the way you wish to be treated. It encourages pure compassion. Think about that the next time you encounter the fund-raising groups in front of your local grocery store or a needy person on the street or even a coworker who asks for your advice.

What if you were to begin viewing these situations as opportunities to show the same kindness, generosity, and compassion that you would like to receive?

But the Golden Rule doesn't stop with those who might merely inconvenience you; it includes your enemies. And is there any tougher commandment than "Love your enemies"? Not tolerate them or simply do kind things for them. Love them. Those obnoxious, cruel, hateful people. The boss who treats you unfairly. The neighbor who pretends to be your friend, then backstabs you. The unhappy customer who maliciously criticizes you and reports you to your superiors. The relative who is consistently rude and hateful.

The first step in loving your enemies is praying for them (not for their disgrace, downfall, or destruction, by the way). And when you pray for your enemies, you need to pray as much for your own attitudes and behaviors as for theirs. That way, even if your prayers don't change your enemies' ugly qualities, they will change yours.

Often, the first thing to pray for is simply the will and grace to want to love those you find unlovable, to show compassion to the uncompassionate.

In praying for these people, you may come to realize that they are loved by God just as much as you are. Further, as you experience what hard work it is to love unlovable people, you will value God's love for you more than ever.

Practice "doing unto others." Some may believe the Golden Rule is out of date, but it's as good as gold.

I Will

Make the Golden Rule a hallmark of my life.

yes   *no*

Trust Jesus' promise that if I show compassion to others companion will be shown to me.

yes   *no*

Prevent myself from keeping score in my relationships with family, friends, and coworkers.

yes   *no*

Pray for the will to show compassion toward difficult people.

yes   *no*

Try to view others through Jesus' eyes.

yes   *no*

Ask for forgiveness when I behave in an unloving, uncompassionate way.

yes   *no*

Follow the example of compassionate people I know.

yes   *no*

Things to Do

☐ *Read Romans 12 for a biblical perspective on compassion.*

☐ *Memorize the Golden Rule in the Bible translation of your choice (Luke 6:31, Matthew 7:17).*

☐ *Find someone you admire as a model of compassion and write him or her a letter of thanks and encouragement.*

☐ *Write a letter or send a card to someone you know who needs a touch of compassion.*

☐ *Sign up to sponsor a needy child through Compassion International, World Vision, or other organization.*

☐ *The next time you encounter a reputable fund-raising group in front of a grocery store, make a donation.*

Things to Remember

Jesus said, "Whatever you want men to do to you, do also to them, for this is the Law and the Prophets."

MATTHEW 7:12 NKJV

Jesus said, "When you give a feast, invite the poor, the maimed, the lame, the blind. And you will be blessed, because they cannot repay you; for you shall be repaid at the resurrection of the just."

LUKE 14:13–14 NKJV

He who has pity on the poor lends to the LORD, and He will pay back what he has given.

PROVERBS 19:17 NKJV

When Jesus went out He saw a great multitude; and He was moved with compassion for them, and healed their sick.

MATTHEW 14:14 NKJV

In the Parable of the Good Samaritan, Jesus said, "A man was going down from Jerusalem to Jericho, and fell among robbers, and they stripped him and beat him, and went away leaving him half dead. . . . But a Samaritan, who was on a journey, came upon him; and when he saw him, he felt compassion . . . and took care of him."

LUKE 10:30, 33–34 NASB

There is no wilderness so terrible, so beautiful, so arid, so fruitful, as the wilderness of compassion. It is the only desert that shall truly flourish like a lily.

—THOMAS MERTON

Until he extends his circle of compassion to include all living things, man will not himself find peace.

—ALBERT SCHWEITZER

Taking Care of Business

Whatever you do, do it heartily, as to the Lord and not to men.
—COLOSSIANS 3:23 NKJV

On the job. It's where you spend the lion's share of your waking hours. And, if you work late at night, you might have spent a few of your sleeping hours at work as well. Many men spend more time at the job than they do with their families, enjoying leisure pursuits, or dozing contentedly in their beds.

Consider this: If you begin a full-time, 40-hour-a-week career at age 22 and retire at age 65, you will spend the equivalent of 3,440 24-hour days on the job. That's 9.5 round-the-clock years of nothing but work—no vacations, holidays, breaks, lunches, or sick time. If you are a salaried professional associate, increase that total by 25 percent to accommodate your 50-hour workweeks. If you're a small-business owner, increase it by 50 percent. Research indicates you are probably putting in 60-hour weeks.

This information doesn't need to be depressing. If you can glean as much wisdom, joy, laughter, skill, and satisfaction as possible on the job, you'll feel better about the hours you put in. Further, if you view God as the One you truly serve, you will find a deeper sense of purpose in your job. And you'll be more likely to attack your daily tasks with perseverance, creativity, diplomacy, efficiency, and teamwork.

If you're still skeptical, it might be worth asking yourself if you are truly in the job God wants you to have. God has given every person unique gifts and talents. Ask yourself if your job is allowing you to exercise yours.

Give yourself this quick test. It will help you discern if you are in the ideal place:

• Does your job allow you to do what you do best—at least some of the time?

• Most of the time, do you approach work with a sense of purpose and excitement—or is your approach more like boredom and dread?

• Do you find that your values mirror those of your company?

• Do you get regular affirmation about the quantity and quality of the work you do—from coworkers, managers, or customers?

• Does your job allow you to provide for your basic needs, and the needs of those who depend on you?

This test isn't a magic formula to determine if you are in the right place, but if you can't give a positive answer to even one or two of the questions above, it might be worthwhile to prayerfully consider other options.

In today's economy, even a bad job might seem better than no job at all, but look at the beginning of this meditation again and consider how much of your life is spent "taking care of business."

Then, think about the gifts God has given you. Keep in mind that God never makes a mistake. His gifts are never the wrong size or style or inappropriate in any way. No one has ever needed to return a gift from God. If you open your heaven-sent gifts, you can then use them in a way that will benefit others and bring glory to your Creator. Do you know what your true gifts are? Are you using them on the job? Or are they lying dormant, gathering dust?

The truth is that these questions and the test above will most likely only confirm what you already know in your heart. If that is to assure you that you are doing what God wants you to do, happily exercising the gifts God has given you, you are most fortunate. Take time to rejoice in that knowledge and thank God.

If you are ready to acknowledge that you are misplaced, don't rashly jump ship. Instead, take time to seek God and ask Him to show you how to find the place He has ordained for you. Ask those close to you to pray as well. As you pray, prepare. Set some money aside, look into career aptitude testing, check out interesting opportunities, open your mind to new ideas, and open your heart to change.

Putting your God-given talents to work is one of the most satisfying things you can do. As you do what God created you for, you gain a deep sense of purpose and become closer and more grateful to the One who gave you your talents. Few things are as beautiful as Creator and creation working together.

I Will

View God as my ultimate boss and strive to serve
Him as I serve others. _____ yes _____ no

Develop an attitude of expectancy about my work. _____ yes _____ no

Bring skill, enthusiasm, and a positive attitude to
my job. _____ yes _____ no

Pray for the wisdom and grace to deal with
challenges on the job. _____ yes _____ no

Be a good on-the-job ambassador for my faith. _____ yes _____ no

Be an encouraging, dependable associate, giving
extra effort to support those who work with me. _____ yes _____ no

Things to Do

☐ *Read Ecclesiastes 5:18–19 for a biblical perspective on work.*

☐ *Memorize Colossians 3:23—"Whatever you do, do it heartily, as to the
Lord and not to men."*

☐ *Start a discussion group or Bible study with some of your coworkers.*

☐ *Drop someone a note of encouragement the next time you see him or
her applying faith on the job.*

☐ *In the next six months, visit a career counselor to help determine if
you are in the right job.*

☐ *Keep a Bible or inspirational book in your work area, to help you keep
work in its proper perspective—and to refer to when you need to make
a difficult decision.*

Things to Remember

He who has a slack hand becomes poor, but the hand of the diligent makes rich.

PROVERBS 10:4 NKJV

Be diligent to know the state of your flocks, and attend to your herds; for riches are not forever, nor does a crown endure to all generations.

PROVERBS 27:23–24 NKJV

The hand of the diligent will rule, but the lazy man will be put to forced labor.
—Proverbs 12:24 NKJV

The plans of the diligent lead surely to plenty, but those of everyone who is hasty, surely to poverty.

PROVERBS 21:5 NKJV

A man's gift makes room for him, and brings him before great men.

PROVERBS 18:16 NKJV

The lazy man does not roast what he took in hunting, but diligence is man's precious possession.

PROVERBS 12:27 NKJV

Work with a smile on your face, always keeping in mind that no matter who happens to be giving the orders, you're really serving God. Good work will get you good pay from the Master, regardless of whether you are slave or free.

EPHESIANS 6:7–8 THE MESSAGE

As for every man to whom God has given riches and wealth, and given him power to eat of it, to receive his heritage and rejoice in his labor—this is the gift of God.

ECCLESIASTES 5:19 NKJV

Let him who stole steal no longer, but rather let him labor, working with his hands what is good, that he may have something to give him who has need.

EPHESIANS 4:28 NKJV

We urge you, brethren, that you increase more and more; that you also aspire to lead a quiet life, to mind your own business, and to work with your own hands, as we commanded you, that you may walk properly toward those who are outside, and that you may lack nothing.

1 THESSALONIANS 4:10–12 NKJV

Work becomes worship when done for the Lord.

—AUTHOR UNKNOWN

Hard work is a thrill and a joy when you are in the will of God.

—ROBERT A. COOK

Fulfillment

You Never Had It So Good

He said to me, "My grace is sufficient for you, for my power is made perfect in weakness." Therefore, I will boast all the more gladly in my weaknesses, so that Christ's power may rest on me.
—2 CORINTHIANS 12:9 NIV

Scan the bestsellers section of a bookstore. Browse your local grocer's magazine aisle. Watch the infomercials on late-night television. You'll find all kinds of so-called sure means to lasting happiness and fulfillment in life—motivational speakers who promise personal empowerment and success in almost any area of life, psychologists who advocate achieving a higher plane of consciousness, psychics who claim the ability to predict and help shape your future.

If you're like most men, you might shake your head in skepticism at all the lofty promises. But the books and articles wouldn't be published—and the infomercials wouldn't be produced and broadcast—if a lot of people weren't buying the advice.

But think about it: If all those methods really worked, everyone would eventually be happy, and there would be no need to keep making new products—or updating the old ones—in order to help people reach fulfillment. If the claims were valid, you would be seeing fewer articles, books, and other products, not more and more.

In truth, there has been only one flawless book on fulfillment—that wonderful sense that you are loved, that your life has meaning and purpose, and that you have what you need to be truly happy. That book is called the Bible. In His Word, God explains true fulfillment: It's realizing that every person is God's workmanship, created to do good works that God Himself has planned. It's experiencing God's love, and then sharing that love with others. It's being grateful for what you have—and for what you do not have.

That last part is something all the fulfillment gurus don't understand. They all point to someone—often themselves—as a model of happiness. The implicit message is to be like them. They play on people's jealousy—their desire to have what someone else has.

God dislikes jealousy, so much that it made His ultimate top-10 list—the Ten Commandments. He etched in stone the following words: "You shall not covet your neighbor's wife, nor his male servant, nor his female servant, nor his ox, nor his donkey, nor anything that is your neighbor's" (Exodus 20:17 NJKV).

In modern terms, this commandment from the book of Exodus could read, "You shall not covet your coworker's salary, your neighbor's home, your brother-in-law's physique, or your best friend's talent."

All people are God's children, and none should compare their blessings with those of others. When you envy what others have, you rob yourself of the joy and contentment you should find in what God gives you. The emotion of jealousy is so powerful that it overtakes and squelches the positive energy you could be using to better yourself.

Guard your heart. If you find yourself unable to rejoice in the success of others, beware. Instead of focusing on what others have, ask God to remind you of the many fulfilling blessings, gifts, and talents He has given you—and how many of them are undeserved.

Further, be open to how God can work through a weakness or lack in your life to achieve His purposes and bring His power to your life. World champion cyclist Lance Armstrong has said that cancer was "the best thing that ever happened to me." He said that he would not have won the Tour de France had he not endured his battle with a life-threatening illness. Former major league pitcher Dave Dravecky wouldn't have begun his ministry to cancer victims and amputees had he not been among their ranks himself. And speaker/artist/author/singer Joni Eareckson Tada, who is also quadriplegic, once told a hushed convention audience, "I would rather be in this wheelchair and know God than have a perfectly healthy body and not know Him."

If you seek true fulfillment, realize that God loves you completely. Know that He has a plan for your life. As you assess your weaknesses, those things that seem to keep you from being happy, be open to how God can use weakness to make His power perfect. Be open to what God is trying to teach you about yourself and about Him. Be open to the ministry opportunities that come your way because of your weakness. Think about how you can encourage others who face the same struggles you do.

I Will

Remember that true fulfillment in life comes from
being loved by God and sharing His love with others. _____yes_____ _____no_____

Be thankful for all that God has given me. _____yes_____ _____no_____

Avoid comparing myself to others. _____yes_____ _____no_____

Ask forgiveness when I find myself growing
greedy or envious. _____yes_____ _____no_____

Avoid chasing after find-fulfillment-now schemes. _____yes_____ _____no_____

Be open to how God might show His strength in my
weakness. _____yes_____ _____no_____

Things to Do

☐ *Memorize Psalm 145:19—"He will fulfill the desire of those who fear Him."*

☐ *Read Ecclesiastes 2 for a biblical portrait about what is—and is not— truly important in life.*

☐ *Write a prayer to God, focusing on a weakness of yours. Ask God what He can teach you through this weakness and how He might show His power through it.*

☐ *Create a list of things you have to be thankful for, things that fulfill you. Review this list periodically and thank God for what He has given you.*

☐ *Using the Bible as a model, write your personalized definition of true happiness and fulfillment.*

Things to Remember

Oh, taste and see that the LORD is good; blessed is the man who trusts in Him! . . . Those who seek the LORD shall not lack any good thing.

PSALM 34:8,10 NKJV

Command those who are rich in this present age not to be haughty, nor to trust in uncertain riches but in the living God, who gives us richly all things to enjoy.

1 TIMOTHY 6:17 NKJV

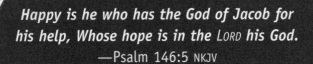

Happy is he who has the God of Jacob for his help, Whose hope is in the LORD his God.
—Psalm 146:5 NKJV

He who heeds the word wisely will find good, and whoever trusts in the LORD, happy is he.

PROVERBS 16:20 NKJV

You will show me the path of life; in Your presence is fullness of joy; at Your right hand are pleasures forevermore.

PSALM 16:11 NKJV

He satisfies the longing soul, and fills the hungry soul with goodness.

PSALM 107:9 NKJV

Bless the LORD, O my soul, and forget not all His benefits. . . . who satisfies your mouth with good things, so that your youth is renewed like the eagle's.

PSALM 103:2, 5 NKJV

Delight yourself also in the LORD, and He shall give you the desires of your heart.

PSALM 37:4 NKJV

May He grant you according to your heart's desire, and fulfill all your purpose.

PSALM 20:4 NKJV

You have caused men to ride over our heads; we went through fire and through water; but You brought us out to rich fulfillment.

PSALM 66:12 NKJV

He will fulfill the desire of those who fear Him; He also will hear their cry and save them.

PSALM 145:19 NKJV

The eyes of the LORD are on the righteous, and His ears are open to their cry.

PSALM 34:15 NKJV

Find satisfaction in him who made you, and only then find satisfaction in yourself as part of his creation.

—AUGUSTINE OF HIPPO

Fulfillment of your destiny does not come in a moment, a month, or a year, but over a lifetime.

—CASEY TREAT

Leadership

Your Actions Lead Better than Words

The LORD said to Joshua, "No man shall be able to stand before you all the days of your life: as I was with Moses, so I will be with you. I will not leave you nor forsake you."

—JOSHUA 1:5 NKJV

John Wooden is a college basketball legend. During his years at UCLA, his teams won a host of national titles. Losses were rare for Wooden's Bruins, and he coached many players, including Bill Walton and Kareem Abdul-Jabbar, who went on to become NBA superstars.

Many factors contributed to Wooden's success. He was a student of the game. He had an eye for talent. He was a great motivator.

However, when former players talk about the privilege of playing for Coach Wooden, they reveal the true key to his effectiveness as a leader: He led by example. One of his most famous axioms was "I never ask a player to do anything— during a game or in practice—that I haven't done myself." Because of this, his players knew that any drills Coach Wooden put them through were for their benefit, and that he wasn't asking them to do something impossible.

Wooden didn't order his players to maintain their composure during games while he screamed at officials, threw chairs, or manhandled a confused point guard. He was an intense competitor, but he didn't let his intensity make him do something foolish that would embarrass him or cost his team a game.

Ben Franklin was another wise man who understood that an ounce of leading by example was worth ten pounds of leading by pressure and intimidation. At one point in his life, Franklin wanted his city, Philadelphia, to lighten up. He believed that lighting the city's streets would not only improve the town aesthetically but also make it safer. But he didn't try to persuade Philly's citizens by talking to them. Instead, he hung a beautiful lantern near his front door. He kept the lantern brightly polished and carefully and faithfully lit the wick each evening just before dusk.

People strolling the dark street saw Franklin's light from a long way off. They found its glow to be friendly and beautiful—and a helpful, guiding landmark. Soon, Franklin's neighbors began placing lanterns in front of their own homes. Before long, the whole city was dotted with light, and more and more people began to appreciate the beauty and value of Franklin's bright idea.

Just as Franklin and Wooden became points of light, your actions can become beacons for those around you—children, employees, fellow church members, and so on. What they see, they copy. And when they see the light of your good example, they may be inspired to illuminate a candle of their own.

I Will

Remember that leadership is more about action than mere rhetoric.

yes   no

Strive to be a consistent, reliable example to those I wish to lead.

yes   no

Emulate the character of great religious, business, and political leaders.

yes   no

Weigh my leadership decisions against the Bible to make sure they are sound and pleasing to God.

yes   no

Be a humble leader, never taking my authority for granted or abusing it.

yes   no

Confess my mistakes, realizing that this honesty will build my credibility with those I lead.

yes   no

Things to Do

☐ *Memorize Colossians 4:1—"Masters, give your bondservants what is just and fair, knowing that you also have a Master in heaven."*

☐ *Read the Gospel of John and note the attributes that made Jesus such an effective leader.*

☐ *Keep a leadership journal, chronicling your leadership successes and setbacks.*

☐ *Create a checklist of the qualities of a great leader; measure yourself against this list periodically.*

☐ *Thank God for providing His Son, a beautiful example of servant leadership.*

☐ *During the next year, attend a workshop or symposium on leadership.*

Things to Remember

Jesus said, "You are the light of the world. . . . Let your light so shine before men, that they may see your good works and glorify your Father in heaven."

MATTHEW 5:14, 16 NKJV

Jesus said, "Whoever desires to become great among you shall be your servant. And whoever of you desires to be first shall be slave of all. For even the Son of Man did not come to be served, but to serve, and to give His life a ransom for many."

MARK 10:43–45 NKJV

A man is known by his actions. An evil man lives an evil life; a good man lives a godly life.

PROVERBS 21:8 TLB

Let us stop just saying we love people; let us really love them, and show it by our actions.

1 JOHN 3:18 TLB

Christ . . . is your example. Follow in his steps: He never sinned, never told a lie, never answered back when insulted; when he suffered he did not threaten to get even; he left his case in the hands of God who always judges fairly.

1 PETER 2:20–22 TLB

> **True greatness, true leadership, is achieved not by reducing men to one's service but in giving oneself in selfless service to them.**
>
> **—OSWALD SANDERS**

> **Although potential leaders are born, effective leaders are made.**
>
> **—BENNIE E. GOODWIN**

One of God's Puzzle Pieces

Trust in the LORD with all your heart, and lean not on your own understanding; in all your ways acknowledge Him, and He shall direct your paths.

—PROVERBS 3:5–6 NKJV

Have you ever neared the completion of a huge jigsaw puzzle, only to find one piece missing? If the puzzle is complex, with 1,000-plus pieces, it's not complete even though the other 999 pieces are all present and accounted for. In fact, the empty space for the missing piece stands out.

When the pieces tumbled from the box, they all seemed equal in value. Many of them shared a color or pattern, making them easy to group together so that a puzzle-solver could get a fast start. All the pieces were important at the beginning of the process. But at the near-completion stage, it's a different story. One missing piece can grab all the attention because a puzzle is always a puzzle without it.

Perhaps you have wondered how you fit in the grand puzzle of life. Maybe you are unlike the other "pieces" around you. They seem to fit in, while you struggle. In fact, you might wonder if you are even part of the puzzle at all.

You are. God has designed every person with unique gifts and unique roles. The Bible doesn't talk about puzzles, but it does inspire the same concept by comparing God's followers to parts of a body. Some parts are larger than others, and they have roles that seem more crucial to the body's health and effectiveness. But *seem* is the key word.

At times you might feel that you are just a little toe and those around you are the arms, legs, heart, and brain. But where would the body be without the little toe? A ranch hand who accidentally shot off his small toe while cleaning a gun found out. He discovered that he couldn't balance well when he attempted to walk and run. And, as other parts of his body tried to compensate for the missing toe, he suffered from cramps and aches in his feet, legs, back, and even up to his neck.

Finally, the toe-less ranch hand had to go to a physical therapist to relearn the art of walking, something he once took for granted. And even with hours of physical therapy and various inserts in his shoe, he was never quite the same without that one-inch baby toe.

However small or insignificant you might seem, you are needed. You are created in God's image, and He has equipped you to carry out your role in His body. Look at the verse that begins this insight passage. If you wholeheartedly seek God's will and appreciate all that He has given you, He will lead you straight down the path of fulfillment and purpose.

Don't worry about being too small a part of the body to make any difference. Every part is necessary for the body to function smoothly and efficiently. Besides, small doesn't mean insignificant. In the Old Testament, God used a tiny army of Israelites to defeat a horde of Midianites. He fed a multitude of people with one boy's small lunch. And He sent a tiny baby to save the world.

It's possible that you never have stopped to consider what part of the body you are—small or big. If that's the case, ask God to show you. Begin by evaluating those things that you are naturally good at. Perhaps you find yourself offering a word of encouragement to others. Or you find that you are especially good at communicating with children or with new believers. Do you prefer to work behind the scenes, making others feel comfortable and taking care of their needs? Do you sing or play an instrument? It could be that you feel most comfortable when you are praying—for the world, for your country, for your community, for those around you.

God is eager to show you where you fit into His big picture. He will be delighted to help you find His will for your life. Just ask Him. Then listen and watch and reach out. Soon you will know with certainty just what role you were intended to play.

God loves you, and He wants you to trust Him to guide your life and take faithful steps—even if they're small ones— that bring you closer to Him every day.

Brothers and sisters, you are holy partners in a heavenly calling. So look carefully at Jesus, the apostle and chief priest about whom we make our declaration of faith.

—Hebrews 3:1 GOD'S WORD

I Will

Acknowledge my key role in God's divine plan.

yes _no_

Seek God's wisdom as I set the course for my life.

yes _no_

Thank God for what He has made me—and not complain that I'm not someone or something else.

yes _no_

Determine to help others find their rightful place in the puzzle of life.

yes _no_

Look for ways that I can support other members of God's body.

yes _no_

Ask for forgiveness when I become jealous of another person's role or status.

yes _no_

Things to Do

☐ *Make a list of my strengths and weaknesses and meditate on what they tell me about my role as part of the body of Christ.*

☐ *Find a person whose part is similar to mine. Commit to encouraging this person and going to him or her for advice.*

☐ *The next time you do a puzzle—or see someone else doing one—stop and thank God for the interrelated roles He has given each person.*

☐ *Memorize Matthew 23:12—"Whoever exalts himself will be humbled, and he who humbles himself will be exalted."*

☐ *Read 1 Corinthians 12, which provides an overview of the body of Christ and the importance of each part.*

☐ *Read an article about someone you believe to be the same part that you are.*

Things to Remember

The eye cannot say to the hand, "I have no need of you"; nor again the head to the feet, "I have no need of you." No, much rather, those members of the body which seem to be weaker are necessary.

1 Corinthians 12:21–22 NKJV

We ask God to give you a complete understanding of what he wants to do in your lives, and we ask him to make you wise with spiritual wisdom.

Colossians 1:9 NLT

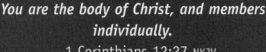

You are the body of Christ, and members individually.
—1 Corinthians 12:27 NKJV

Having then gifts differing according to the grace that is given to us, let us use them.

Romans 12:6 NKJV

The Lord is my shepherd . . . . He leads me in the paths of righteousness for His name's sake.

Psalm 23:1, 3 NKJV

I love to do God's will so far as my new nature is concerned.

Romans 7:22 TLB

Ananias said to Paul, "The God of our fathers has chosen you that you should know His will, and see the Just One, and hear the voice of His mouth."

ACTS 22:14 NKJV

Jesus said, "Anyone who does God's will is my brother, and my sister, and my mother."

MARK 3:35 TLB

A man's heart plans his way, but the LORD directs his steps.

PROVERBS 16:9 NKJV

There are many plans in a man's heart, nevertheless the LORD's counsel—that will stand.

PROVERBS 19:21 NKJV

The steps of a good man are ordered by the LORD, and He delights in his way.

PSALM 37:23 NKJV

Paul and Timothy wrote: We also pray that you will be strengthened with glorious power so that you will have all the patience and endurance you need. May you be filled with joy.

COLOSSIANS 1:11 NLT

Inside the will of God there is no failure. Outside the will of God there is no success.

—BENARD EDINGER

God's will is our peace and there is no other peace. God's service is perfect freedom and there is no other freedom.

—FATHER ANDREW

Finances

Become the Richest Man in the World

On the first day of every week, each one of you should set aside a sum of money in keeping with his income, saving it up, so that when I come no collections will have to be made.

—1 CORINTHIANS 16:2 NIV

Open the pages of a men's magazine and note what's being advertised: luxury cars, sports cars, digital TVs, computers that fit in the palm of your hand, plastic surgery, thousand-dollar suits, Swiss watches.

Many American men, it seems, have a possession obsession. And while there's nothing inherently wrong with wanting fine clothes, state-of-the-art business accessories, or cool sports equipment, material goods can easily become a source of false security, even pride.

The same danger exists with money. Many men strive to earn bonuses, get maximum profit sharing, and beef up their 401k accounts. "More" never seems to be "enough." Are you satisfied with your present earnings? Do they cover all your expenses? Are you able to save as much for the future as you'd like? Or do you crave a substantial raise and hope to get to the next level, the next plateau on Money Mountain?

The ultimate test of your success in life is not how much wealth and possessions you can amass. On the contrary, Jesus taught His followers to travel light, taking with them only what they would need for their journey. He reminded them to concentrate on God's divine love, which provides a richness unmatched by any worldly possession. This love is so brilliant that it makes everything else pale in comparison. Materialism, on the other hand, is excess baggage that in the end only serves to make the journey burdensome.

To help them travel light, Jesus taught His followers to give. When we give to others out of our time, money, and resources, Jesus says that we are giving to Him—not as if we are giving to Him, but in fact are giving to Him.

Do you want to become a truly rich man? Don't encumber yourself with possessions you don't need. Don't be consumed with getting to the next tax bracket. Focus on traveling light and giving freely. After all, material possessions can be stolen or destroyed. Retirement funds can shrink. Jobs can be lost.

But the caring and compassion that you give to others can make a lasting impact. A few people may be impressed by or envious of a man's material wealth. Their lives, however, can be deeply enriched by his generosity.

Think about your life's goals and priorities. Do you want to be known or remembered for how much you saved or for how much you gave?

I Will

Remind myself often that all I have, or ever will have, has come from God.

    yes   *no*

Strive to develop a thankful heart, by taking time each day to thank God for all He has given me, both materially and spiritually.

    yes   *no*

Focus on what I truly need in life, not what I want.

    yes   *no*

Seek God's wisdom as I evaluate my purchases and investment decisions.

    yes   *no*

Avoid comparing my salary, home, car, etc., to someone else's.

    yes   *no*

Ask God to forgive me for the times I have let greed creep into my heart.

    yes   *no*

Things to Do

☐ *Conduct a personal financial audit to determine what percentage of your discretionary income is going to charity.*

☐ *Do a thorough spring cleaning of your residence (even if it's not spring). Collect unneeded items to donate to a local charity or school.*

☐ *Memorize Hebrews 13:5—"Let your conduct be without covetousness; be content with such things as you have."*

☐ *Within the next year, attend a biblically based workshop on financial management.*

☐ *Read the book of Ecclesiastes and note Solomon's ultimate verdict on material wealth.*

☐ *Write a note of encouragement to someone you see giving to others in a Christ-like manner.*

Things to Remember

Jesus said to them, "Take heed and beware of covetousness, for one's life does not consist in the abundance of the things he possesses."

LUKE 12:15 NKJV

Let each one give as he purposes in his heart, not grudgingly or of necessity; for God loves a cheerful giver.

2 CORINTHIANS 9:7 NKJV

"Bring all the tithes into the storehouse, that there may be food in My house, and try Me now in this," says the LORD of hosts, "If I will not open for you the windows of heaven and pour out for you such blessing that there will not be room enough to receive it."

MALACHI 3:10 NKJV

Honor the LORD with your possessions, and with the firstfruits of all your increase; so your barns will be filled with plenty, and your vats will overflow with new wine.

PROVERBS 3:9–10 NKJV

The love of money is a root of all kinds of evil, for which some have strayed from the faith in their greediness, and pierced themselves through with many sorrows.

1 TIMOTHY 6:10 NKJV

God made man to be somebody, not just to have things.

—AUTHOR UNKNOWN

If a person gets his attitude toward money straight, it will help straighten out almost every other area in his life.

—BILLY GRAHAM

Worry

No Need to Sweat It

Jesus said, "Do not worry about tomorrow, for tomorrow will worry about its own things. Sufficient for the day is its own trouble."

—MATTHEW 6:34 NKJV

Worry. It can be like a giant python. Your doubts about your abilities, your uncertainty about others' feelings toward you, your anxieties about what might happen in the future—they become like reptilian coils that surround you and squeeze the energy and hope out of you. The more you struggle against them, the tighter those coils constrict.

Want to avoid the crushing, oppressive power of a python called worry? Want to keep your anxieties from dominating your life? You have two weapons at your disposal: The first is perspective; the other is peace. Think of them as two clubs you can use to beat that worrisome snake on the head the next time it tries to capture you in its grip.

The apostle Paul, who wrote much of the Bible's New Testament, was a man who had perspective. He instructed fellow believers to be "anxious for nothing." He didn't give this advice flippantly. He was in prison at the time he wrote it. In fact, he spent a lot of time in various "gray-bar motels," where he was beaten, clasped in chains, and separated from those he loved.

Beyond these trials, Paul had some type of thorn in the flesh, a physical condition that pained him so much that he asked God repeatedly to cure him. God, in this case, said no.

When he wasn't in jail, Paul was getting shipwrecked, bitten by poisonous snakes, and pelted with stones by people who didn't appreciate his outspoken faith. Ultimately, his belief in God got him beheaded.

So, when a guy like this tells you not to worry, you should listen. And you should emulate the kind of perspective he had. Paul knew what was truly important. He knew God loved him and had a plan for his life.

God loves you too. He has a plan for your life, and that plan doesn't include being consumed by worry. So maintain the right perspective. Will the world stop turning if you don't quite make that deadline or don't get a hoped-for promotion? Will babies no longer giggle and birds no longer sing if your company's net revenues don't meet budget or you don't lose the ten pounds you hope to shed this year?

What is a traffic ticket or flat tire or late report or missed deal or cold sore or reprimand from a manager compared with being loved purely and eternally by Almighty God and being made clean from all of your sins?

Paul operated his life from this kind of heavenly perspective—a perspective that gave him peace, despite all the painful trials he endured. As Paul learned, God won't always untie all the knots in your life—those things that make you worry. But the heavenly Father does give you the grace to live with the knots.

There is nothing you face that is too difficult, too troubling, or too frightening for God. God doesn't have sweat glands. Problems don't keep Him up at night—He's awake and on the job all the time.

Use this knowledge of God's power to transform worry time into triumph time, the way Paul did.

When he was in jail, for example, instead of worrying about how he was being treated or when he would be released, he wrote letters of encouragement and instruction to large groups of believers and individual friends. He sang hymns of praise to God. In at least one case, he led his jailer to a saving faith in God.

You can follow Paul's lead. If, for example, you've heard that your company might downsize in the future, don't spend your days and nights fretting over what might happen. Do your best work. Determine an action plan in the event you are affected. Help your colleagues develop action plans of their own. Be someone with whom they can share their fears and anxieties. Encourage one another. It's amazing how helping others can eliminate worry and stress.

The next time you feel worry closing in on you, remember the message that Paul, the physically impaired, oft-jailed martyr preached: The Lord is nearby. Don't worry about anything. Simply pray and be thankful as you present your needs to God. This will give you peace—more peace than you can imagine—and that peace will guard your heart and your mind as you trust in Jesus your Lord.

I Will

Maintain a positive, hopeful outlook about life, regardless of circumstances.

yes _no_

Transform worry time into productive prayer time.

yes _no_

Avoid worrying about things that are beyond my control.

yes _no_

Share my worries with God and trust Him to guide me through worrisome times.

yes _no_

Reach out to people who worry, helping them deal with the trials they face.

yes _no_

Things to Do

☐ _Turn to God first the next time you are faced with worry._

☐ _Buy or borrow a Christian book on the topic that worries you most._

☐ _Write down an action plan about something that worries you—and start carrying it out._

☐ _Read Matthew 6 to get Jesus' perspective on worry._

☐ _Watch a comedy TV show or movie the next time you feel worry creeping up on you._

☐ _Memorize Psalm 31:19—"How great is Your goodness, which You have laid up for those who fear You, which You have prepared for those who trust in You in the presence of the sons of men!"_

Things to Remember

May God bless you richly and grant you increasing freedom from all anxiety and fear.

1 Peter 1:2 TLB

Jesus said to His disciples, "Therefore I say to you, do not worry about your life, what you will eat; nor about the body, what you will put on. Life is more than food, and the body is more than clothing."

Luke 12:22–23 NKJV

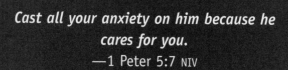

Cast all your anxiety on him because he cares for you.
—1 Peter 5:7 NIV

Don't worry about anything; instead, pray about everything; tell God your needs, and don't forget to thank him for his answers.

Philippians 4:6 TLB

In the multitude of my anxieties within me, your comforts delight my soul.

Psalm 94:19 NKJV

Search me, O God, and know my heart; try me, and know my anxieties; and see if there is any wicked way in me, and lead me in the way everlasting.

Psalm 139:23–24 NKJV

Anxiety in the heart of man causes depression, but a good word makes it glad.

PROVERBS 12:25 NKJV

Do not be afraid of sudden terror, nor of trouble from the wicked when it comes; for the LORD will be your confidence, and will keep your foot from being caught.

PROVERBS 3:25–26 NKJV

Don't fret and worry—it only leads to harm.

PSALM 37:8 TLB

Don't shuffle along, eyes to the ground, absorbed with the things right in front of you. Look up, and be alert to what is going on around Christ—that's where the action is. See things from his perspective.

COLOSSIANS 3:1–2 THE MESSAGE

The LORD said, "Fear not, for I am with you; be not dismayed, for I am your God. I will strengthen you, yes, I will help you, I will uphold you with My righteous right hand."

ISAIAH 41:10 NKJV

Worry does not empty tomorrow of its sorrow; it empties today of its strength.

—AUTHOR UNKNOWN

Tomorrow has two handles: the handle of fear and the handle of faith. You can take hold of it by either handle.

—AUTHOR UNKNOWN

Listening to God

Hear the Still Small Voice

Hear, O my people, and I will speak.

—Psalm 50:7 NIV

Today's fast-paced society is filled with noise. Cell phones jangling. Tires squealing. Babies screaming. Sirens blaring. Music pounding. Advertisers shouting. With all that competes for our attention—and shatters our concentration—it's no wonder most people have a hard time hearing God's voice. Some may reach the conclusion that God isn't communicating, but the gap exists at the human end, not the divine one. God is always speaking—reaching out—but we are not always listening.

It's impossible to have a close relationship without communication, and listening is vital to communication. We must listen to God if we want to understand how He feels about us and how He wants us to live. He might not speak with a thundering voice from the heavens anymore, but neither is He silent. His voice is no less clear than it ever was. You may hear it through the advice of a friend, a Scripture passage, a song on the radio, even the words of a child.

Here are three ideas for improving your listening-to-God skills, in several different aspects of your spiritual life.

1. When you read your Bible, make it a focused, interactive experience. Eliminate distractions. For example, don't read a few verses during commercial breaks while watching your favorite TV show. Approach the privilege of Bible-reading with a clear mind and an open heart. Think deeply about each word you read. Be willing to learn something new; be open to discover something you've missed before. Be willing to change as a result of what you read.

As you read, think about how you can apply the words— immediately and practically—to your life. Write down any action steps you plan to take. Underline or highlight passages you want to memorize. If you come to a passage that is confusing or troubling, highlight that as well and plan to ask a pastor or other spiritual mentor about it. Pray about what you read. Ask God for the wisdom to truly understand His Word— and the courage and perseverance to live by biblical principles.

Don't think of your Bible as some ancient artifact or conversation piece. Think of it as a hotline to God's wisdom and love. The power of God's message doesn't reside in an impressive leather binding or pages gilded with gold, but in the Bible's ability to transform your heart, mind, and soul.

2. When you pray, take time, and take care. Are your prayers quick monologues to God or true conversations with Him? Prayer is as much about listening to God as it is about speaking to Him. It might be tempting to hit God with a barrage of requests, utter a few thank-yous, and then hurry on to the next order of the day. This is not true prayer.

True prayer is unhurried. It's communion with your heavenly Father, the creator of the universe. So slow down. Approach God in prayer with quietness and reverence. Pay attention to what He might be telling you. The Bible says that if we are in tune with God, our own hearts can instruct us. Be open when you pray. What is God saying to your heart?

3. Consider meditating. You might be uncomfortable with the term *meditation*. It might evoke images of bearded gurus, garbed in camelhair robes, sitting cross-legged in a circle and chanting meaningless monosyllables. Not so. To meditate means, simply, to think deeply and continuously about something.

If you want to listen more closely to the voice of God, meditation can mean focusing on one particular Bible verse, and pondering what it says about God's character and His feelings toward humanity. It can mean thinking about God's goodness, His kindness. It can mean taking time to appreciate what God has done in your life, the way He's guided your steps, protected you from harm, provided for your needs.

Do all you can to be more attentive to God. It can make the difference between just knowing about God and truly knowing Him personally. That's a difference that will transform your life and bring you hope for tomorrow and courage for today. That difference can and will transform your life.

Now that you have made me listen, I finally understand.

—Psalm 40:6 NLT

I Will

Keep my mind and heart open to God.   _yes_   _no_

Follow Jesus' perfect example of listening to God's
voice and following His direction.   _yes_   _no_

Avoid multitasking when it comes to my
spiritual life.   _yes_   _no_

Ask forgiveness for the times I've ignored God.   _yes_   _no_

Insist on devoting quality time to God every day.   _yes_   _no_

Study the Bible with a humble heart and a mind
eager to learn.   _yes_   _no_

Things to Do

- [ ] *Read Hebrews 3:7–19 for biblical insights on hearing God's voice.*

- [ ] *For the next month, practice eliminating all noise and distraction from your prayer and devotional time. Note the difference it makes.*

- [ ] *Find someone you admire as a model follower of God and write him or her a letter of thanks and encouragement.*

- [ ] *Create a list of ten things you can do to become closer to God, then follow through.*

- [ ] *Memorize Proverbs 1:5—"A wise man will hear and increase learning."*

- [ ] *Make a list of the ways you feel God can communicate to you (through Christian music and books, a pastor's teaching, a friend's advice, even a sunset or rainbow). Use the list to enhance your communication and closeness with your creator.*

Things to Remember

We also thank God without ceasing, because when you received the word of God . . . you welcomed it not as the word of men, but as it is in truth, the word of God, which also effectively works in you who believe.

1 THESSALONIANS 2:13 NKJV

He who looks into the perfect law of liberty and continues in it, and is not a forgetful hearer but a doer of the work, this one will be blessed in what he does.

JAMES 1:25 NKJV

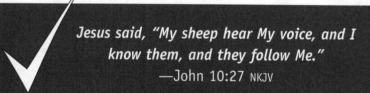

Jesus said, "My sheep hear My voice, and I know them, and they follow Me."
—John 10:27 NKJV

Your ears shall hear a word behind you, saying, "This is the way, walk in it," whenever you turn to the right hand or whenever you turn to the left.

ISAIAH 30:21 NKJV

Thus says the LORD, your Redeemer, the Holy One of Israel: "I am the LORD your God, who teaches you to profit, who leads you by the way you should go."

ISAIAH 48:17 NKJV

The LORD will guide you continually, and satisfy your soul in drought, and strengthen your bones; you shall be like a watered garden, and like a spring of water, whose waters do not fail.

ISAIAH 58:11 NKJV

Jesus said, "To him the doorkeeper opens, and the sheep hear his voice; and he calls his own sheep by name and leads them out. And when he brings out his own sheep, he goes before them; and the sheep follow him, for they know his voice."

JOHN 10:3–4 NKJV

Jesus said, "When He, the Spirit of truth, has come, He will guide you into all truth; for He will not speak on His own authority, but whatever He hears He will speak; and He will tell you things to come."

JOHN 16:13 NKJV

When I remember You on my bed, I meditate on You in the night watches. Because You have been my help, therefore in the shadow of Your wings I will rejoice.

PSALM 63:6–7 NKJV

God never ceases to speak to us, but the noise of the world without and the tumult of our passions within bewilder us and prevent us from listening to him.

—FRANÇOIS FÉNELON

If you keep watch over your hearts, and listen for the voice of God and learn of him, in one short hour you can learn more about him than you could learn from man in a thousand years.

—JOHANN TAULER

Identity

Do You Know Who You Are?

Put on the new man, which was created according to God, in true righteousness and holiness.

—EPHESIANS 4:24 NKJV

A man with what he thought was an amazing replica of a Leonardo da Vinci painting took his work of art to a museum. He showed the copied painting to the curator to get his reaction. The curator immediately identified the painting as a forgery—and also hypothesized about the identity of the copyist, his nationality, and when the copy was made.

Then the curator turned the painting over. The information on the back confirmed that he was right on all three counts. "How did you know it was a fake?" the man asked. "It looks like an amazing likeness to me."

"People who make a living copying the masters have little imagination of their own," the curator explained. "And this person's choice of subject, brush strokes, and areas of emphasis practically scream 'Fake!' Think about those celebrity impersonators, how they overemphasize a certain vocal inflection, facial expression, or gesture. It's the same thing here."

Whatever your calling in life, you may be tempted to copy the successful people in your field. But the best one can hope for with this approach is the moniker Master Imitator, not Master Artist, Musician, Writer, or whatever. True, many take the well-traveled path; that's why we have six *Police Academy* movies and only one *Casablanca*. But this road doesn't lead to greatness or pride in one's work.

If you truly want to distinguish yourself, be an innovator, not an imitator. God has given you unique skills, ideas, and experiences. There is no one just like you anywhere on the planet. Take some time to think about the characteristics that make you, you! Write them down on a piece of paper and keep it with you. Work on only one characteristic at a time. If it is a positive quality—something you like about yourself— ask God to help you find new ways to nurture and express it. Then seek out opportunities to exercise that trait in the service of others.

If the quality is something you would consider negative— something you dislike about yourself—ask God to show you how to turn a liability into an asset. For example, if you have trouble being still, ask God to help you seek out opportunities to use your extra energy to help others.

Most of all, remember that there's only one way to be a true original in this copycat world: Be yourself.

I Will

Strive to maintain my individuality, resisting the pressure to conform.

yes _____ *no* _____

Thank God for making me a unique creation.

yes _____ *no* _____

Do and say what is right and true, not necessarily what is popular or trendy.

yes _____ *no* _____

Pray for the courage to be an individual.

yes _____ *no* _____

Periodically check my speech, dress, and behavior to ensure I'm avoiding conformity.

yes _____ *no* _____

Make a point to warn the children in my life about the dangers of nameless, faceless conformity and encourage them to live out and celebrate their unique God-given gifts.

yes _____ *no* _____

Things to Do

☐ *Memorize Ephesians 2:10—"We are His workmanship, created in Christ Jesus for good works, which God prepared beforehand that we should walk in them."*

☐ *Read an article by or about a strong, unique individual you admire.*

☐ *Make a list of the positive qualities that make you an individual and separate you from the pack. Check yourself against this list at least once a year.*

☐ *Read Romans 12:1–8 for a biblical model of individuality.*

☐ *Ask your spouse or a trusted friend about what makes you a true individual in his or her eyes—then work on building these traits.*

Things to Remember

In Him we live and move and have our being.

ACTS 17:28 NKJV

We are His workmanship, created in Christ Jesus for good works, which God prepared beforehand that we should walk in them.

EPHESIANS 2:10 NKJV

There are diversities of gifts, but the same Spirit. There are differences of ministries, but the same Lord. And there are diversities of activities, but it is the same God who works all in all.

1 CORINTHIANS 12:4–6 NKJV

Just as there are many parts to our bodies, so it is with Christ's body. We are all parts of it, and it takes every one of us to make it complete, for we each have different work to do. So we belong to each other, and each needs all the others.

ROMANS 12:5 TLB

You formed my inward parts; You covered me in my mother's womb. I will praise You, for I am fearfully and wonderfully made; marvelous are Your works, and that my soul knows very well.

PSALM 139:13–14 NKJV

Be what you are. This is the first step toward becoming better than you are.

—JULIUS CHARLES HARE AND AUGUSTUS WILLIAM HARE

Meeting people unlike oneself does not enlarge one's outlook; it only confirms one's idea that one is unique.

—ELIZABETH BOWEN

Blessings

Count 'Em and Leap

Many, O Lᴏʀᴅ my God, are Your wonderful works which You have done; and Your thoughts toward us cannot be recounted to You in order; if I would declare and speak of them, they are more than can be numbered.

—Psᴀʟᴍ 40:5 ɴᴋᴊᴠ

There's a peppy little hymn from the late 1800s written by Johnson Oatman Jr. titled "When upon Life's Billows" or, as it is more commonly known, "Count Your Blessings." No matter how low or discouraged you feel beforehand, once you start singing that song, you'll probably forget why you had been in such a funk.

When you name and count your blessings—and there are many of them—it's clear to see how God touches your everyday life. How many can you count just in the last day or so? Perhaps you avoided a collision with a car that ran a red light; perhaps an honest clerk noticed you gave him a twenty instead of a five; perhaps you were running late for an important business meeting and, miraculously, a malfunction in the video equipment delayed the meeting's start by fifteen minutes; perhaps the new product manager expressed interest in the idea that you've been working on for the past year; perhaps your loved one kissed you and told you just how much you mean to her.

But it's sometimes too easy to forget the wondrous everyday blessings when unending responsibilities and things to do demand your attention. You may slip into a sort of selective amnesia, forgetting the positive and only seeing the negative—problems, shortcomings, great needs. What happens? Just as Peter took his eyes off Jesus and began to sink, so you may begin to sink when you take your eyes off your blessings.

It's not hard to remember the bad things you encounter or the things lacking in your life—humans are naturals at that—and society doesn't help much. Your neighbor's new car reminds you of your old one. Your kids don't seem satisfied with what you bought them. Commercials tell you that you need to get rid of your gray hair, join a fitness club, lose some weight, grow greener grass . . . The list goes on.

Let the words of that hymn remind you that you must focus on your blessings, keeping them at the forefront of your mind. When your mind focuses on the negative, you tend to feel bad; but when you focus on the positive, you feel good. That is why Norman Vincent Peale's *The Power of Positive Thinking* was so popular, even though its message is so simple.

The next time you start feeling down—or, better yet, while things are good—think of all the things God has given you. You will see how much better off you are than you ever imagined.

I Will

Choose to smile more often.   _yes_   _no_

Recognize the little things in life that bring
me joy.   _yes_   _no_

Be happy for others when good things
happen to them.   _yes_   _no_

Expect to find the silver lining and the pot of gold.   _yes_   _no_

Be a positive-thinking man.   _yes_   _no_

Thank God for what He has done, and is doing,
in my life.   _yes_   _no_

Believe that God can turn any negative
into a positive.   _yes_   _no_

Things to Do

☐ Sing, or simply read, some hymns of blessings and thankfulness.

☐ Check out books on how things work, such as phones, automobile
engines, and sump pumps.

☐ Write thank-you cards to friends and family—just because they've been
so good to you.

☐ If you have an office assistant, pitch in with the filing one day to
show your appreciation.

☐ Thank God for the things you take for granted, such as color pens, a
thesaurus, paper towels, remote controls, and smoke alarms.

☐ Put up a sheet of paper on the fridge for a week and see how many
blessings you can come up with—be ready to add a second sheet.

Things to Remember

As you abound in everything—in faith, in speech, in knowledge, in all diligence, and in your love for us—see that you abound in this grace also.

2 CORINTHIANS 8:7 NKJV

Thank the God of all gods, his love never quits.

PSALM 136:2 THE MESSAGE

Offer to God thanksgiving, and pay your vows to the Most High.

PSALM 50:1 NKJV

Sing to the LORD, bless His name; proclaim the good news of His salvation from day to day. Declare His glory among the nations, His wonders among all peoples.

PSALM 96:2–3 NKJV

Every creature of God is good, and nothing is to be refused if it is received with thanksgiving.

1 TIMOTHY 4:4 NKJV

Continue earnestly in prayer, being vigilant in it with thanksgiving.

COLOSSIANS 4:2 KJV

Lord, dismiss us with thy blessing,
Hope, and comfort from above;
Let us each, thy peace possessing,
Triumph in redeeming love.

—ROBERT HAWKER

In each event of life, how clear
Thy ruling hand I see!
Each blessing to my soul more dear,
Because conferred by Thee.

—HELEN MARIA WILLIAMS

New Life

Happy Birthday to You

If anyone is in Christ, he is a new creation; old things have passed away; behold, all things have become new.

—2 CORINTHIANS 5:17 NKJV

A Russian boy plagued by feelings of ugliness gazed into a mirror and studied his reflection—wide nose, thick lips, tiny gray eyes, over-large hands and feet. The boy was so distraught about his appearance that he begged God to work a miracle and transform him into a handsome man. He vowed that if God would re-create him, he would give his Creator all that he now possessed, and all that he would earn in the future.

That Russian boy was Count Tolstoy, who grew up to become one of the world's most revered authors. He is best known for his epic *War and Peace*. In another of his books, Tolstoy revealed that through the years, he discovered that the physical beauty he once craved is not the only beauty in life. Nor is it the best kind of beauty. Ultimately, Tolstoy grew to regard the beauty of strong character as being most pleasing to God's eyes. With that realization came a true rebirth in Tolstoy's life.

Once his eyes were opened to what is truly important

in life, he wrote with a new sense of passion, care, and boldness, and he portrayed in his books the importance of courage and conviction, not that of fleeting physical beauty.

Many people today spend vast sums on their physical appearance. They will follow any solution that promises "a new you." Expensive business suits. Tanning sessions at the spa. Gold watches. Cosmetic surgery. But these accouterments can't truly renew a person; they can only cover up or attempt to reshape aging flesh and bone.

Godly character, in contrast, can't be bought or applied or worn. When God enters a man's heart, he works a transformation from the inside. Being a Christian doesn't give you younger-looking skin or whiter teeth. But it does give you a fresh perspective on life. It helps you realize what truly matters. That realization guides you as you seek to discover where to invest your time and talents.

Further, being renewed by God provides the character and courage to do what is good, to stand up for what's right. It gives birth to the qualities that you can't see by looking into the mirror. Those are the qualities that truly matter, because physical beauty will ultimately fade. Spiritual beauty, conversely, endures forever.

Don't become too occupied with the war on physical decay. Focus instead on the peace and purpose that come from being a born-again child of God. Make today your birthday—or your re-birthday.

I Will

Allow God to renew me from the inside out.   *yes*   *no*

Remind myself that God is concerned with the state of my heart, not my receding hairline.   *yes*   *no*

Avoid judging others based on their clothing or physical attractiveness.   *yes*   *no*

Spend more time on my inner character than my outward appearance.   *yes*   *no*

Look for areas of my life in which I need a fresh start.   *yes*   *no*

Avoid spending too much of my money on look-younger products.   *yes*   *no*

Things to Do

☐ *Read Matthew 23:25–28 to get Jesus' perspective on those who obsess over external appearance.*

☐ *Memorize Romans 12:2—"Do not be conformed to this world, but be transformed by the renewing of your mind."*

☐ *Find a person with whom you can be mutually accountable as you strive to build a new life based on godly character.*

☐ *Write a note of thanks to someone who is a shining example of a new creation.*

☐ *Over the next month, track the amount of time you spend working on your outer self (gym time, grooming time, and so forth) and the amount of time you invest on your inner character.*

Things to Remember

O man of God . . . pursue righteousness, godliness, faith, love, patience, gentleness. Fight the good fight of faith, lay hold on eternal life, to which you were also called and have confessed the good confession in the presence of many witnesses.

1 TIMOTHY 6:11–12 NKJV

Lie not one to another, seeing that ye have put off the old man with his deeds; and have put on the new man, which is renewed in knowledge after the image of him that created him.

COLOSSIANS 3:9–10 NKJV

We all, with unveiled face, beholding as in a mirror the glory of the Lord, are being transformed into the same image from glory to glory, just as by the Spirit of the Lord.

2 CORINTHIANS 3:18 NKJV

Do not be conformed to this world, but be transformed by the renewing of your mind, that you may prove what is that good and acceptable and perfect will of God.

ROMANS 12:2 NKJV

> The first time we're born, as children, human life is given to us; and when we accept Jesus as our Savior, it's a new life. That's what "born again" means.
> —JIMMY CARTER

> Christian experience is not so much a matter of imitating a leader as accepting and receiving a new quality of life.
> —H. A. WILLIAMS

Encouragement

Fill Up Your Empty Tank

The LORD is my strength and my song, and He has become my salvation.

—PSALM 118:14 NKJV

Scott was in trouble. With still a couple of miles to go in a grueling forty-mile bicycle ascent of a steep Colorado mountain, his strength, his patience, his enthusiasm—and his water—were gone. Every grueling downstroke on the pedals felt as if it would be his last. He prayed silently for some reserve of energy to kick in.

He thought about dismounting and attempting to walk the rest of the way, but two miles was a long way to tread in bicycle shoes. He thought about the other members of his cycling group—probably already checked into a hotel on the other side of the mountain pass, enjoying the late afternoon sun—the same sun that was beating down on Scott, burning his skin and sapping what little energy he had left.

Then, suddenly, Scott felt a surge of momentum. It felt as if a benevolent hand was pushing him up the hill. He turned to his left. A cyclist with weather-bronzed skin had reached out his right hand and was gently pushing Scott forward.

"You look like you could use a little boost," the cyclist said. "And I heard you coughing. Are you out of water?"

Scott nodded. He was too parched to speak.

"Pull over to the side for a minute," the cyclist instructed. "I've got just the thing to recharge your batteries."

As Scott sat on the roadside, gulping a sports drink and munching an energy bar, the cyclist checked his bike over, then filled one of Scott's water bottles to the halfway mark. Then, once Scott was back in the saddle, his newfound friend gave him a running push start. "Keep working," he heard the cyclist call after him, "it's only a mile and a half to the summit, then it's all downhill. You can do it!"

Refreshed and reenergized by the kindness that had been shown to him, Scott churned his way to the top. As he sped down the other side of the mountain, he wondered if he had encountered an angel. *Nah. Angels don't wear cycling helmets and Lycra bike shorts, do they?*

God promises rest and replenishment for the weary. This refreshment can take many forms—even that of a benevolent stranger. Don't hesitate to ask God for His gifts of strength and renewal. Your gift might take the form of a spiritual retreat at a local conference center, an inspiring worship service, an afternoon away from work lying on your couch and listening to soothing music, or a basketball game in the driveway.

Whatever the solution, pull over to the side of the road and let God refresh you mentally, physically, and spiritually. You'll be amazed at how much more ground you can cover when your tank is on *F* and not *E*.

I Will

Take the time to let God reenergize me when I begin
to feel run-down.   *yes*   *no*

Be aware of signs that indicate I am weary—
physically, mentally, and spiritually.   *yes*   *no*

Be watchful for unexpected ways that God can use to
refill my tank when it nears the empty point.   *yes*   *no*

Say no to demands that will deplete me and hamper
my ability to be at my best.   *yes*   *no*

Avail myself of the benefits of quiet prayer times and
moments of personal worship and meditation.   *yes*   *no*

Things to Do

- [ ] *Within the next year, plan to attend a spiritual-refreshment seminar or retreat at a Christian conference center.*

- [ ] *Purchase a few CDs of your favorite style of soothing, inspirational music, which you can play when your nerves are frayed and your body is weary.*

- [ ] *Keep a spiritual journal, noting the times you have become weary, and how God gave you new strength.*

- [ ] *Attend a concert or speech by a favorite inspirational artist, group, or speaker.*

- [ ] *Make a date for a night out with friends.*

- [ ] *Memorize Proverbs 11:25—"The generous soul will be made rich, and he who waters will also be watered himself."*

Things to Remember

We do not lose heart. Even though our outward man is perishing, yet the inward man is being renewed day by day.

2 CORINTHIANS 4:16 NKJV

Those who wait on the LORD shall renew their strength; they shall mount up with wings like eagles, they shall run and not be weary, they shall walk and not faint.

ISAIAH 40:31 NKJV

He will not break the bruised reed, nor quench the dimly burning flame. He will encourage the fainthearted, those tempted to despair.

—ISAIAH 42:3 TLB

Jesus said, "These things I have spoken to you, that in Me you may have peace. In the world you will have tribulation; but be of good cheer, I have overcome the world."

JOHN 16:33 NKJV

My flesh and my heart fail; but God is the strength of my heart and my portion forever.

PSALM 73:26 NKJV

Encouragement costs you nothing to give, but it is priceless to receive.

—AUTHOR UNKNOWN

Encouragement is oxygen to the soul.

—GEORGE M. ADAMS

Love for Your Wife

Love that Lasts a Lifetime

Many waters cannot quench love, neither can floods drown it. If one offered for love all the wealth of one's house, it would be utterly scorned.

—SONG OF SOLOMON 8:7 NRSV

Love used to be so simple when you were younger, wasn't it? As a third-grader, you knew that the big deal about love was reserved for one day out of the year—Valentine's Day. You'd go with your mom to the five-and-dime and buy dozens of brightly colored glossy cards with cute sentiments and give one to everyone in your class. At school that day, you'd eat a cupcake or two, maybe talk a little about the holiday and how it got started. But that was it. Nothing to it. No stress. No effort. No problem. Nothing really personal about it.

If you're married now, though, your wife expects much more than a cupcake and a card once a year—and it needs to be a whole lot more personal. Valentine's Day for a married couple can be thought of as a year-round event. Sounds like a lot of pressure on a guy. Sure, you want your wife never to doubt your love, but is it possible to show that kind of love 24/7? Actually, yes—if you believe that God put you two together, that He took the two of you and made you one flesh.

God wants you two to grow closer and closer to each other. One way to do that is to romance your wife, no matter how many years you have been married. Think back to the days when you were courting your wife. You called her frequently, you wrote her notes, you sent her flowers, you walked hand in hand wherever you went. Hold on to those early feelings of courtship.

It will take a little effort on your part, but the rewards are worth it. Call her from work and ask her out. Take her to her favorite restaurant for dinner or pack a picnic supper and take it to the park. Take a short walk with her every night when the sun is starting to set. It isn't so much *what* you do as *that* you do. What matters to her is seeing that you care.

Don't let anything keep you from spending quality time with your wife. Consider this: Back when you were dating, would you have let another man ask out your girlfriend? No way! The Bible says that God is a jealous God when it comes to His relationship with you, and that is how valued He wants you to consider your wife.

I Will

Make building a stronger marriage a high priority.　　_yes_　　_no_

Know we were made for each other because God joined us together.　　_yes_　　_no_

Seek God's blessing on my marriage.　　_yes_　　_no_

Put my wife first—above our children, my friends, and my work.　　_yes_　　_no_

Treat my wife the way I treated her on our first date.　　_yes_　　_no_

Look for ways to encourage my wife.　　_yes_　　_no_

Love my wife as God commanded.　　_yes_　　_no_

Things to Do

☐ *Write a note to your wife and mail it to her.*

☐ *Recreate your first date.*

☐ *Compliment your wife at least once in the morning and once at night.*

☐ *Make some popcorn and sit down to watch your wedding video together.*

☐ *Read the Song of Solomon together.*

☐ *Tell your wife about how you are doing and feeling; don't just give her recaps of your day's events.*

☐ *Pray for your wife's needs and for her spiritual growth daily.*

Things to Remember

You are like a private garden, my treasure, my bride! You are like a spring that no one else can drink from, a fountain of my own. You are like a lovely orchard bearing precious fruit, with the rarest of perfumes.

SONG OF SOLOMON 4:12 NLT

Let him kiss me with the kisses of his mouth—for your love is better than wine.

SONG OF SOLOMON 1:1 NKJV

Husbands, go all out in your love for your wives, exactly as Christ did for the church—a love marked by giving, not getting. Christ's love makes the church whole. His words evoke her beauty.

EPHESIANS 5:25–26 THE MESSAGE

Kissing you is more delicious than drinking the finest wine. How wonderful and tasty!

SONG OF SONGS 7:9 CEV

A man shall leave his father and mother and be joined to his wife, and the two shall become one flesh.

MATTHEW 19:5 NKJV

Your love is better than wine.

SONG OF SOLOMON 1:2 NKJV

If ever two were one, then surely we.

If ever man were loved by wife, then thee;

If ever wife was happy in man,

Compare with me ye women if you can.

—ANNE BRADSTREET

Familiar acts are beautiful through love.

—PERCY BYSSHE SHELLEY

Answered Prayer

God's Timing Is Perfect

You see, at just the right time, when we were still powerless,
Christ died for the ungodly.

—ROMANS 5:6 NIV

We live in an age of immediate gratification. Instant messaging. Instant coffee. Instant breakfast. Instant rice. In today's world, you can get quality eyeglasses in less than an hour or a hot, fresh pizza delivered to your door in less than thirty minutes. People today demand quickness and convenience, and usually get it. However, these expectations should not spill over into your spiritual life.

God doesn't work according to human deadlines. His timing isn't always your timing, but it is always perfect. He will answer, and you'll have his answer when you need it.

Mike and his wife tried for years to conceive a child. Even after much prayer and medical intervention, however, they were unsuccessful. Mike was particularly distraught. Since high school, he had dreamed of being a dad. And he was feeling pressure to provide the first grandchild on either side of the family. Worst of all, he felt that he was failing his wife. He couldn't understand why he was being denied his most ardent prayer.

Then Mike's wife began to experience strange physical symptoms. Puzzled, she visited her doctor—and learned she was pregnant. Mike had to restrain himself from whooping out loud when she called him at work to deliver the news. Later that night, as his wife lay asleep beside him, Mike meditated on the many things that had changed since they had first asked God for a child.

First, they were in a new home, which was larger and in a better neighborhood. Second, Mike had a better job that paid more, required less travel, and was more stable. Third, and perhaps most important, Mike felt that he was more mature, wise, and settled in his marriage. He knew he was better equipped to handle the challenges—and appreciate the joys— of being a father and supporting his wife in her role.

No matter what you may be praying about, God hears your prayer. Sometimes his answer is no, sometimes yes, and sometimes wait. You can be assured that God will answer you according to his infinite wisdom, impeccable timing, and boundless love.

If you feel that God is giving you a no answer, think about what He might be trying to teach you. Think about how what you want might not be what you need, at least at the present moment—because what seems like a "no," might well be a "wait." If that is the case, you will discover, just as Mike and Tammy did, that the wait will be worth it.

I Will

Remind myself that God's timing is always perfect
and that mine is not.

yes *no*

Strive to view God as my heavenly Father, not
merely a prayer-answering machine.

yes *no*

Be grateful for God's answers to my prayers, even
when the answer is "no" or "wait."

yes *no*

Be open to what God is trying to teach me through
His answers to my prayers.

yes *no*

Realize that God always has my best interests at
heart when He answers my prayers.

yes *no*

Be watchful for the unexpected ways that God
might answer my prayers.

yes *no*

Things to Do

☐ *The next time you pray, thank God for the specific prayers He has
answered for you in the past few months.*

☐ *During the coming year, attend a workshop, retreat, or Sunday-school
series on prayer and patience.*

☐ *Keep a prayer journal, noting requests to God and how and when they
were answered.*

☐ *Read Matthew 6:9–13 and meditate on Jesus' words in the Lord's
Prayer.*

☐ *The next time God answers one of your prayers, thank Him
immediately.*

Things to Remember

He has made everything beautiful in its time.

ECCLESIASTES 3:11 NKJV

"My thoughts are not your thoughts, nor are your ways My ways," says the LORD. "For as the heavens are higher than the earth, so are My ways higher than your ways, and My thoughts than your thoughts."

ISAIAH 55:8 NKJV

Lead me in Your truth and teach me, for You are the God of my salvation; on You I wait all the day.

PSALM 25:5 NKJV

Wait on the LORD; be of good courage, and He shall strengthen your heart; wait, I say, on the LORD!

PSALM 27:14 NKJV

Now I know that the LORD saves His anointed; He will answer him from His holy heaven with the saving strength of His right hand.

PSALM 20:6 NKJV

By awesome deeds in righteousness You will answer us, O God of our salvation, You who are the confidence of all the ends of the earth, and of the far-off seas.

PSALM 65:5 NKJV

God will always answer our prayers; but he will answer them in his way, and his way will be the way of perfect love.

—WILLIAM BARCLAY

Keep praying, but be thankful that God's answers are wiser than your prayers!

—WILLIAM CULBERTSON

Marriage

Maintaining a Magnetic Marriage

The wife does not have authority over her own body, but the husband does. And likewise the husband does not have authority over his own body, but the wife does.

—1 CORINTHIANS 7:4 NKJV

God could have used any number of analogies to illustrate His relationship with His followers: employer-employee, teacher-student, athlete-coach, even master-slave. But the one He chose was groom-bride. Clearly, the relationship between husband and wife is important to Him.

Further evidence of God's high esteem for the concept of marriage can be found throughout the Bible. The New Testament, for example, is filled with words of advice for how a husband should treat his wife. In fact, in New Testament times, the condition of a man's marriage was a major criterion in determining if he was fit to be a leader in the church.

When you praise, compliment, care for, and celebrate your spouse, you are honoring a relationship created by

God Himself. And as you build a loving, mutually respectful marriage partnership, you gain a deeper understanding of the kind of relationship God wants to have with you.

God is with you for the long haul. He won't give up on you, even when you disobey or disappoint Him. He wants you to have that same attitude. Marriage should be a commitment, not an experiment. In Hollywood, some stars change spouses as frequently as they change the oil in their BMWs; you need a scorecard to track who is divorcing and who is marrying, remarrying, or re-remarrying.

God holds people to a higher standard. True, there are times when ending a marriage is the least damaging solution, but is it ever the best solution? God is forgiving and patient with His people, and married men and women would do well to exercise those traits in their relationships.

Think of your marriage as a triangle, its sides composed of you, your spouse, and God. As long as the sides stay connected to each other, the triangle will have balance and stability. Only when a side loses touch can the integrity and strength of the triangle be compromised.

So divorce yourself from anything that threatens to come between you, your spouse, and your God. Commit yourself fully to her, just as God has committed Himself fully to you. Learn to listen to your wife and treat her lovingly and considerately, just the way God treats you. When there are differences and disputes bring them to God together. Be willing to let God open your heart and shine His light on the issue in question. Determine that you will be slow to anger and quick to forgive. Most of all, ask God to help you love your wife without measure, just as He loves you.

I Will

Remember always that marriage is an institution established and honored by God.

yes   *no*

Not allow popular culture's disrespect or ambivalence toward marriage color my view of my relationship with my wife.

yes   *no*

Seek God's wisdom as I strive to be a great husband.

yes   *no*

Pray for my marriage and my spouse every day.

yes   *no*

Realize that my performance as a husband can affect my children's perspective on the institution and, perhaps, influence their choice of a spouse someday.

yes   *no*

Things to Do

☐ *Within the next year, find an exemplary husband you can emulate and whom you can go to for advice and support.*

☐ *This month, surprise your wife with a special date or weekend getaway.*

☐ *Memorize Ephesians 5:33—"Let every one of you in particular so love his wife even as himself."*

☐ *During the next month, begin a time of prayer and devotions with your wife.*

☐ *Look at your calendar and pick a day on which you will send your wife flowers or some other indulgence to show your love for her.*

☐ *Read 1 Corinthians 13 for a beautiful picture of what true love is.*

Things to Remember

The husband provides leadership to his wife the way Christ does to his church, not by domineering but by cherishing.

EPHESIANS 5:23 THE MESSAGE

Husbands ought to love their own wives as their own bodies; he who loves his wife loves himself. For no one ever hated his own flesh, but nourishes and cherishes it, just as the Lord does the church.

EPHESIANS 5:28–29 NKJV

My beloved brethren, let every man be swift to hear, slow to speak, slow to wrath.

JAMES 1:9 NKJV

Let each one of you in particular so love his own wife as himself, and let the wife see that she respects her husband.

EPHESIANS 5:33 NKJV

A man shall leave his father and mother and be joined to his wife, and they shall become one flesh.

GENESIS 2:24 NKJV

Let your fountain be blessed, and rejoice with the wife of your youth.

PROVERBS 5:18 NKJV

Successful marriage is always a triangle, a man, a woman, and God.
CECIL MYERS

To have and to hold from this day forward, for better for worse, for richer for poorer, in sickness and in health, to love and to cherish, till death us do part, according to God's holy ordinance; and thereto I plight thee my troth.
—THE BOOK OF COMMON PRAYER

Rest

Take a Load Off

"Come to me, all you who labor and are heavy laden, and I will give you rest."

—MATTHEW 11:28 NKJV

God doesn't sweat. He doesn't get tired or suffer from aching muscles. He never gets stressed out, despite the size of a task. He never needs to use aspirin or megavitamins or analgesic ointments. Yet what did he do after creating the world? He rested. He didn't need to rest, but He purposefully took the time to step back, cease working, and enjoy His creation. If God made time to rest, shouldn't you?

As a member of the human race, you need to rest occasionally. You need to focus on the *human*, once in a while, and not so much on the *race*. Take time to recover physically, emotionally, and spiritually from life's demands. Take time to take stock of where you've been, where you are, and where you are headed. Take the time for quiet, reflective, and restful moments—away from stress and to-do lists. Take the time to be a friend, a parent, a child of God.

It's ironic that the animal kingdom understands this

principle. Consider this example: Japan's snow monkeys work hard just to stay alive in their frigid habitat. They must climb high mountains continuously as they search for food. But they take frequent breaks to rest, renew themselves, even monkey around a little. They seem to have an innate understanding that all work and no play leads to exhaustion—and maybe extinction.

The lesson: It's possible to become so obsessed with work that you ignore your body's physical and mental signals that rest and replenishment are needed. It's not wise to disregard those signals. Various studies—including a recent one at the University of Chicago—reveal that those who fail to recharge their mental and physical batteries once in a while are more susceptible to illness and stress-related problems such as ulcers, and to mistakes on the job. Rest can help you avoid such perils.

Additionally, in resting you will find the time and the right frame of mind to contemplate God's wonders and to thank Him for His grace and kindness to you. And you can gather the energy to live your life to the fullest.

There's no question—you need rest to be at your best. But rest can be elusive. How can you fit some downtime into an already-crowded life?

Here are a few tips:

Build rest time into your daily schedule. Let's face it, if you're like many guys, that's the only way you'll refrain from nonstop work and activity. And it's OK to be a bit selfish, a bit inflexible about this rest time. If you aren't selfish, something else will crowd it out. Take a regular twenty-minute walk after lunch, or at mid-afternoon break time. One businessperson goes to his car every afternoon, reclines his seat, and grabs a fifteen-minute power nap.

On a similar line, use your vacation time. All of it. If you're self-employed, give yourself at least a couple of weeks off each year. Go someplace for vacation, even if it's just to a nearby town. If you don't "get out of Dodge," you might find yourself being pulled back into the job. One executive at a large U.S. company makes a point of scheduling vacations in remote areas, where he will be almost impossible to reach—even by cell phone.

Another great way is to pursue interests and hobbies that differ from what you do on the job. And, in this case, adopting a favorite TV show can count as an interest. This strategy can help you engage and feed your brain and body in a way that your job does not. At the same time, it will give those often-used job-related parts a needed respite.

Finally, get adequate sleep at night. Your body needs it. Your mind needs it. Sure, you might be able to get more work done if you sleep fewer hours each night, but at what cost?

To be at your best, to be healthy, to be a well-rounded person, to fully and truly enjoy life, you must find the time to rest your body, mind, and spirit. Think of all the extra hours you spend working. Think of what that time could mean to your family, your well-being, and your relationship with God—the God who understands the value of occasional rest time.

I Will

Appreciate the physical, mental, and spiritual benefits of rest.

_____ yes   _____ no

Trust Jesus' promise that if I ask Him He will give me rest.

_____ yes   _____ no

Insist on having a life and not just a career.

_____ yes   _____ no

Protect my rest time from the intrusion of busy-ness.

_____ yes   _____ no

Seek God's wisdom as I determine my life's priorities.

_____ yes   _____ no

Learn not to expect too much of myself.

_____ yes   _____ no

Things to Do

☐ For the next month, set aside a quiet time each day. Then, consider making this time part of your everyday life.

☐ Over the next week, strive to get at least eight hours of sleep per night. Note the difference it makes in your energy level, thinking ability, and overall outlook on life.

☐ Take all your vacation and holiday time this year.

☐ Look at your daily planner or schedule for the upcoming week. Is it overcrowded with things to do? Eliminate or reschedule the items that are nonessential.

☐ The next time you become sick, take time to recover—and see a doctor if you need to.

Things to Remember

On the seventh day God ended His work which He had done, and He rested on the seventh day from all His work which He had done.

GENESIS 2:2 NKJV

The LORD said, "Remember the Sabbath day, to keep it holy. Six days you shall labor and do all your work, but the seventh day is the Sabbath of the LORD your God. In it you shall do no work."

EXODUS 20:8–10 NKJV

The LORD said, "My Presence will go with you, and I will give you rest."
—Exodus 33:14 NKJV

My people will dwell in a peaceful habitation, in secure dwellings, and in quiet resting places.

JEREMIAH 32:18 NKJV

Thus says the LORD: "Stand in the ways and see, and ask for the old paths, where the good way is, and walk in it; then you will find rest for your souls."

JEREMIAH 6:16 NKJV

The LORD said, "I have satiated the weary soul, and I have replenished every sorrowful soul."

JEREMIAH 31:25 NKJV

The LORD is my shepherd; I shall not want. He makes me to lie down in green pastures; He leads me beside the still waters. He restores my soul.

PSALM 23:1–3 NKJV

Jesus said, "Take My yoke upon you and learn from Me, for I am gentle and lowly in heart, and you will find rest for your souls. For My yoke is easy and My burden is light."

MATTHEW 11:29–30 NKJV

There remains therefore a rest for the people of God. For he who has entered His rest has himself also ceased from his works as God did from His.

HEBREWS 4:9–10 NKJV

Rest in the LORD, and wait patiently for Him; do not fret because of him who prospers in his way.

PSALM 37:7 NKJV

Return to your rest, O my soul, for the LORD has dealt bountifully with you.

PSALM 116:7 NKJV

How beautiful it is to do nothing, and then rest afterward.

—SPANISH PROVERB

Jesus knows we must come apart and rest awhile, or else we may just plain come apart.

—VANCE HAVNER

Contentment

Your Grass Is Really the Greenest

Serving God does make us very rich, if we are satisfied with what we have.

—1 Timothy 6:6 NCV

Most men are competitive at their core. The reason is twofold: one, men love to win; and, two, men hate to lose. Competition is more an issue of contentment than it is a pursuit of victory—a man doesn't want the competition to possess what he doesn't have. Can you relate? But consider this. If God has placed you where He wants you to be and given you what He wants you to have, then perhaps you need to be content and not worry about the other guy.

As you get older, competition shifts from the sports field to the grassy field of your backyard. Sure, you may enjoy working out in the yard, but you may also be motivated by dissatisfaction with the condition of your lawn. You may find yourself believing the cliché that the grass is greener on the other side of the fence. But that couldn't really be true. Right?

Is the grass greener on the other side of the fence? According to James Pomerantz in his scientific article "'The Grass Is Always Greener': An Ecological Analysis of an Old [Saying]" (Perception, 1983), optical and perceptual laws alone can make the neighbor's lawn look greener than the blades of grass perpendicular to the ground that one looks down upon in his own yard.

It's hard to find contentment in your life when you spend too much time looking at what other people have. When that happens, you soon only see what you lack rather than what you are blessed with. That is one of Satan's favorite ploys. One, he wants to pit you against your brothers, and, two, he wants to shift your eyes off what God has done and is doing in your life.

So how can you get past this green-grass fabrication? One thing you can do is to figuratively tear down the fences between you and your neighbors and spend time with each other. See them as allies rather than as rivals. Another thing you can do is to enjoy the grass in your yard. Unless God provides the rain and sun (i.e., unless He wants you to have something you don't right now), then don't worry about it. Ask God to open your eyes to what you have and to give you a spirit of contentment with the beautiful grass under your feet.

I Will

Feel richly blessed because what God has given me. _yes_ _no_

Stop complaining or obsessing over what
I don't have. _yes_ _no_

Believe that God blesses me daily with things that go
unnoticed. _yes_ _no_

Be happy for my neighbor and not envious. _yes_ _no_

See my neighbor as my ally rather than as my enemy. _yes_ _no_

Stop competing and start enjoying life. _yes_ _no_

Know that God withholds some blessings for very
good reasons. _yes_ _no_

Things to Do

☐ Walk barefoot on your lawn, feeling the blades between your toes and noticing the lush green colors.

☐ Walk over to your neighbor's yard and see how similar it is to yours.

☐ Write down things you don't have but wish you did (talents, material possessions, spiritual gifts).

☐ Pray about those things on your list, and cross them off one by one as you give them over to God, knowing that He will give them to you in His perfect time if He wants you to have them.

☐ Walk around your house and thank God for at least ten things He has blessed you with (in your home or your heart).

☐ Take a day off work just to relax at home—don't go anywhere and don't do any chores.

Things to Remember

I have learned how to get along happily whether I have much or little.

PHILIPPIANS 4:11 TLB

Remove falsehood and lies far from me; give me neither poverty nor riches—feed me with the food allotted to me.

PROVERBS 30:8 NKJV

Let your conduct be without covetousness; be content with such things as you have. For He Himself has said, "I will never leave you nor forsake you."

HEBREWS 13:5 NKJV

Better is a little with the fear of the LORD, than great treasure with trouble.

PROVERBS 15:16 NKJV

A little that a righteous man has is better than the riches of many wicked.

PSALM 37:16 NKJV

Again, I saw that for all toil and every skillful work a man is envied by his neighbor. This also is vanity and grasping for the wind.

ECCLESIASTES 4:4 NKJV

To be content is to be happy.

—CHINESE PROVERB

Little I ask; my wants are few,

I only want a hut of stone, (A very plain brownstone will do,) That I may call my own.

—OLIVER WENDELL HOLMES

Faithfulness

You Can Always Count on Him

It is good to give thanks to the LORD . . . to declare Your lovingkindness in the morning and Your faithfulness at night.

—PSALM 92:2 NKJV

A magazine needed to send a group of rare photographs to its printer. The photos belonged to an aging writer, who had lost the negatives years before. The magazine's staff weighed overnight courier options carefully. They decided to go with a different carrier from the one they typically used, because this competitor boasted a 99.9 percent delivery record.

The next day, the printer called, noting that the photos had not arrived. Frantic, the magazine's editor had the courier trace the missing package. After two days of searching, a courier representative reported the news: "We simply can't find your package. At this point, we have to assume that it's hopelessly lost—or that it was accidentally destroyed by our machinery in the sorting process."

"But your company touts its 99.9 percent efficiency rating," the editor complained. "How could this happen?"

"Please understand," the rep said calmly, "we do have a high rating. The best in the business. But if we handle a hundred thousand packages in a day, even at 99.9 percent that means that a hundred packages will not make it to their destination. Unfortunately, in this case, your package was part of that minuscule percentage."

Even the best companies can't perform perfectly. None of them is 100 percent dependable, because human beings aren't perfect, and, therefore, neither is the equipment they build and maintain.

Whether in business or at home, people will let you down.

There is only one name that means perfect dependability every time, and it isn't followed by a trademark symbol or a clever logo. What is that name? God.

No matter what the scenario, you can depend on God. The book of Lamentations assures that God's compassion never fails. Job proclaims that God can do all things. And in Psalm 13, David, even in the midst of suffering, vows that he will trust in his heavenly Father's unfailing love.

What security and peace of mind come from trusting in God! In a world where even the people with the best intentions, the purest hearts, and the highest skill levels will fail at some point, those who follow God have a secure rock that they can cling to in times of need or trouble.

The magazine staff learned the truth of human fallibility. Despite their intentions, the photos were lost. The good news is that you can learn from their experience. People and things cannot provide you with true security. That comes only from God. Put your ultimate trust in Him and see what develops.

I Will

Turn to God first in times of need. _yes_ _no_

Thank God regularly for His unwavering faithfulness. _yes_ _no_

Allow God's faithfulness to inspire me to be more
trustworthy in my relationships with others. _yes_ _no_

Ask God's forgiveness when I fail to trust Him. _yes_ _no_

Sincerely thank people when they are trustworthy to
me—keeping promises, following through on
commitments, and so on. _yes_ _no_

Follow Jesus' example of perfect faithfulness and
perfect obedience to His heavenly Father's will. _yes_ _no_

Things to Do

☐ Make a list of times when God has shown His faithfulness to you—and thank Him for it.

☐ Write out a promise to be more trustworthy in a specific area of your life and put it in a prominent place where you will see if often.

☐ Look up the word faithful in a Bible concordance and read every passage listed.

☐ Memorize Psalm 118:8—"It is better to trust in the LORD than to put confidence in man."

☐ Find the dictionary definitions for the word faithful and meditate on how they apply to God.

☐ Using the writings of King David as a model, write your own psalm about God's faithfulness.

Things to Remember

Moses said to the Israelites, "Know that the LORD your God, He is God, the faithful God who keeps covenant and mercy for a thousand generations with those who love Him and keep His commandments."

DEUTERONOMY 7:9 NKJV

Your mercy, O LORD, is in the heavens; Your faithfulness reaches to the clouds.

PSALM 36:5 NKJV

Some trust in chariots, and some in horses; but we will remember the name of the LORD our God.

PSALM 20:7 NKJV

Jesus Christ is the same yesterday, today, and forever.

HEBREWS 13:8 NKJV

Your faithfulness endures to all generations; You established the earth, and it abides.

PSALM 119:90 NKJV

I am the LORD, I change not.

MALACHI 3:6 NKJV

What more powerful consideration can be thought on to make us true to God, than the faithfulness and truth of God to us?
—WILLIAM GURNALL

In God's faithfulness lies eternal security.
—CORRIE TEN BOOM

Serving

Acing Your Serves

You shall fear the Lord your God: you shall serve Him, and to Him you shall hold fast.

—Deuteronomy 10:20 NKJV

Jesus was called a king and a prince, yet He didn't lead a royal life. He didn't have a large staff of personal assistants and servants. He didn't live in a palace. And the only crown He ever wore was made of thorns.

He befriended the outcasts of society, and at least once in His life He got on His hands and knees to wash the feet of His disciples. And keep in mind that these men walked dirty roads in nothing but sandals, didn't have access to showers, and couldn't avail themselves of foot powder or deodorants.

Jesus' life is a great example of servanthood, and it shows that even great leaders are called to be servants. Jesus once told his disciples—who were jockeying for status at the time—that whoever among them wanted to be great should be the servant of all.

Indeed, serving humankind is a divine mandate. God wants His people to serve one another. But it's not always easy to do. Some people won't appreciate your efforts to help them. They might never say a simple thank-you to note your efforts. Perhaps they feel they are entitled to being served, or they may simply be ungrateful.

Other people are hard to serve, because, as you serve them, you get the feeling that they will never reciprocate your kindness. Still others might assign ulterior motives to your efforts to serve them.

Whatever the case, keep on serving—especially those challenging people. If you find your own resentment building, don't focus primarily on serving your fellow men and women. Focus instead on serving the God who loves you unconditionally and sees your efforts. God is your ultimate boss, your ultimate audience. Find your motivation in Him.

Pray that God will help you see others as He sees them— recipients of His grace and love. And then begin to visualize each person you encounter, not as the person you see before you but as a unique individual, created in God's image. Your whole perspective will change.

When your goal is serving God through serving others, you can be assured that however your efforts turn out, He will be proud of you. And there are few joys as deep as those in knowing that you are pleasing your heavenly Father. Give it all you have—ace your serves—for the One who best understands and appreciates the value of service to others.

I Will

Remember that I am called by God to serve others. _yes_ _no_

Follow Jesus' perfect example of servanthood. _yes_ _no_

Keep my pride and ego in check. _yes_ _no_

Behave like a servant even when I don't feel like one—knowing that sometimes attitude follows action. _yes_ _no_

Pray for humility and a servant's heart. _yes_ _no_

Thank those who serve me and let them know how much they are appreciated. _yes_ _no_

Be the first to volunteer for tasks or duties that others might consider beneath them. _yes_ _no_

Things to Do

☐ *Read Ephesians 6:1–9 for biblical insights on being a servant and a faithful worker.*

☐ *Pick a person you will make an extra effort to serve in the coming month—and follow through.*

☐ *Find someone you admire as a model servant and write him or her a letter of thanks and encouragement.*

☐ *Create a list of ten things you can do to become a better servant at home, on the job, and within your church (or other organization you belong to).*

☐ *Memorize Philippians 2:3—"In lowliness of mind let each esteem others better than himself."*

Things to Remember

Serve the LORD with gladness; come before His presence with singing.

PSALM 100:2 NKJV

Whatever you do, do it heartily, as to the Lord and not to men, knowing that from the Lord you will receive the reward of the inheritance; for you serve the Lord Christ.

COLOSSIANS 3:23–24 NKJV

Moses said to the Israelites, "What does the LORD your God require of you, but to fear the LORD your God, to walk in all His ways and to love Him, to serve the LORD your God with all your heart and with all your soul?"

DEUTERONOMY 10:12 NKJV

Jesus said, "Whoever desires to become great among you, let him be your servant . . . just as the Son of Man did not come to be served, but to serve, and to give His life a ransom for many."

MATTHEW 20:26, 28 NKJV

You, brethren, have been called to liberty; only do not use liberty as an opportunity for the flesh, but through love serve one another.

GALATIANS 5:13 NKJV

Down in their hearts, wise men know this truth: the only way to help yourself is to help others.

—ELBERT HUBBARD

Tied to the value of the person is the principle of servanthood. We value what we freely serve.

—DOUGLAS GROOTHUIS

Go the Extra Mile

Love does no harm to a neighbor; therefore love is the
fulfillment of the law.

—ROMANS 13:10 NKJV

A veteran pastor began a custom during his Sunday-morning service—a custom he continued for twelve years. Before dismissing the children for junior church, he invited them all to the front of the sanctuary to march past his pulpit on their way to the special kid-oriented service in the church basement. As the kids walked past him, the pastor made a point to smile lovingly at each one.

One Sunday, however, the pastor became distracted during the youth exodus. He forgot to smile at one curly-haired four-year-old girl. This girl left the line of children and ran back to her mother. Sobbing uncontrollably, she threw herself into her mother's arms.

After the service, the pastor sought out the mother to find out what had happened. She explained to him that, after her child quit crying, she had told her, "Mommy, I'm so sad. I smiled at God, but he didn't smile back at me!"

The pastor reflected, "To that child, I stood for God. I had failed with my smile, and the world went dark for her."

God uses people to express his love here on earth. You might have heard that God's followers are his hands and feet. They are also his smile, his loving voice, and his caring arms.

In one of his most compelling lessons, Jesus taught that when you show love to those who are sick, poor, imprisoned, and hungry, you are reaching out to the Lord Himself. Jesus didn't say, "When you show love to others, it's as if you are loving me." He said, "Assuredly, I say to you, inasmuch as you did it to one of the least of these My brethren, you did it to Me" (Matthew 25:40 NKJV).

This truth means that you must see Jesus in the hungry faces of third-world children, the hopeless eyes of street beggars, even the hardened countenances of convicts. Following this teaching will revolutionize the way you show love to others. Think about it: If you see Jesus in the eyes of a panhandler in front of your local grocery store, can you merely ignore him and hurry by? Can you even just slip him a dollar, while trying not to touch him or look him in the eyes? If this downtrodden person truly represents the Son of God, how can you do anything but take the time to show love, to speak words of encouragement, to ask, "What can I do to help you?"

You can be assured that the kindness you show will make a difference in someone's life. Remember that pastor in the first paragraph? He had a son who became a youth speaker. As he spoke to groups across the country, he invited them to take a short quiz.

First, he asked them to identify the three best sermons

they had ever heard and say why those particular sermons meant so much to them. Few teens could remember even one sermon, not even the one they had heard only a week before, much less name one that had had an impact on their lives.

Next, the speaker asked the teens to name the three people who had made the biggest impact on their lives. This time, no one had any problem coming up with an answer. In fact, the hardest part of this exercise was limiting the list to only three. And the teens did more than list names. They told heartwarming stories of people who had inspired them, guided them in important decisions, comforted them in times of trouble, or showed them kindness when no one else would.

In the Bible, God promises that one's labor in the Lord, is never in vain. Groups of teens across the country are living examples of that truth. One person, reaching out with love to others, can make a difference.

Some might find being God's ambassadors of love to be a chore. In reality, it is a privilege. God has provided a way that you can serve Jesus directly and personally, while also making a difference in the lives of the men, women, and children around you. And, as you give to Jesus by giving to those who need love, you will better appreciate all that God has given you. After all, where would you be today without the love that others have shown to you?

Jesus said, "As the Father loved Me, I also have loved you; abide in My love."

—John 15:9 NKJV

I Will

Determine to make love the cornerstone of my life,
just as God has commanded.

yes   _no_

Love others, without prejudice or concern over
whether they will love me back.

yes   _no_

Show love even to people who are unpleasant to me.

yes   _no_

Pray to God and ask Him to give me a loving heart.

yes   _no_

Let the love I share be an example to others.

yes   _no_

Look for creative, meaningful ways to show love to
others, going the extra mile when necessary.

yes   _no_

Things to Do

☐ _Memorize Mark 12:31—"Love your neighbor as yourself."_

☐ _Make a list of the ways you can show love at home, in your
neighborhood, on the job, and at church. Check yourself against this
list at least once a year._

☐ _Read 1 Corinthians 13 for a biblical model of love._

☐ _Ask someone close to you if you are a loving person and listen carefully
to the response._

☐ _Write your own definition of love. Keep this definition in a
prominent place._

☐ _The next time you encounter a person who is disagreeable to you in
some way, make an extra effort to show love to him or her._

Things to Remember

Jesus said, "Whoever compels you to go one mile, go with him two. Give to him who asks you, and from him who wants to borrow from you do not turn away."

MATTHEW 5:41–42 NKJV

You are our epistle written in our hearts, known and read by all men; clearly you are an epistle of Christ, ministered by us, written not with ink but by the Spirit of the living God, not on tablets of stone but on tablets of flesh, that is, of the heart.

2 CORINTHIANS 3:2–3 NKJV

Jesus said, "Greater love has no one than this, than to lay down one's life for his friends."
—John 15:13 NKJV

Let us love one another, for love is of God; and everyone who loves is born of God and knows God.

1 JOHN 4:7 NKJV

If you love only the people who love you, what praise should you get? Even sinners love the people who love them. . . . But love your enemies, do good to them, and lend to them without hoping to get anything back.

LUKE 6:32, 35 NCV

Love never gives up, never loses faith, is always hopeful, and endures through every circumstance.

1 CORINTHIANS 4:7 NLT

If God so loved us, we also ought to love one another. . . . If we love one another, God abides in us, and His love has been perfected in us.

1 JOHN 4:11–12 NKJV

If someone says, "I love God," and hates his brother, he is a liar; for he who does not love his brother whom he has seen, how can he love God whom he has not seen? And this commandment we have from Him: that he who loves God must love his brother also.

1 JOHN 4:20–21 NKJV

Let all that you do be done with love.

1 CORINTHIANS 16:14 NKJV

The LORD said to Moses, "Don't seek vengeance. Don't bear a grudge; but love your neighbor as yourself, for I am Jehovah."

LEVITICUS 19:18 TLB

Walk in love, as Christ also has loved us and given Himself for us, an offering and a sacrifice to God for a sweet-smelling aroma.

EPHESIANS 5:2 NKJV

To love another person is to help them love God.

—SØREN KIERKEGAARD

Love is a condition in which the happiness of another person is essential to your own.

—ROBERT HEINLEIN

Strength

Let God Pump You Up

God is my strength and my power, and He makes my way perfect.

—2 Samuel 22:33 NKJV

For most men, the pursuit of strength begins in childhood. It's the result of a man's God-given instinct to be self-sufficient and able to defend himself and others. So where should a man look for strength? Where do you look?

When Charles Atlas arrived in America in 1903, he weighed only ninety-seven pounds and bullies often took advantage of him. In an effort to overcome this problem, he began to exercise regularly and use techniques gathered from boxing, wrestling, and karate.

His personal program worked so well that he decided to market it to the public in 1928. The advertising campaign depicted a bully kicking sand into the face of a skinny, young kid. Vowing revenge, the skinny kid sends away for the Atlas program and returns to the beach several months later as a bulked-up hulk. When the bully starts to act up again, he socks him a good one as crowds of onlookers cheer him on. He had gone from wimp to the hero of the beach.

Young men everywhere bought into the message that physical strength leads to personal power and prestige, and within months, Charles Atlas was a millionaire. Today, this message still prevails. Americans dropped nearly $5.8 billion on home exercise equipment in the year 2000, and health-club memberships rose to an all-time high of 32.8 million.

Certainly, the idea that increased physical strength will give you power and control over your life is an alluring one. But the problem is, there will always be someone stronger. Physical strength just isn't enough.

What you really need is God—the ultimate strongman. He never grows weary, and His strength can sustain you long after your power gives out. When you walk with God and rely on Him, He will build you up and make you into a powerhouse for His kingdom. You will no longer have to fear anyone or anything, for there is no situation too big for Him to handle.

Keep in mind that, just as growing physical muscles takes effort, so does growing spiritual muscles. You will need to train by reading God's Word and seeking Him regularly through prayer. However, as you quit trying to get through the struggles in life by your own efforts and start relying on God's supreme power, He will build you up day by day. As you grow in the Lord, some of those things that seemed so tough in the past will soon seem like nothing at all.

I Will

Accept the fact that I have weaknesses.   _yes_ _no_

Allow God to show me where I need his strength.   _yes_ _no_

Believe that God will empower me when I am weak.   _yes_ _no_

Accept God's strength in my life.   _yes_ _no_

Remind myself that I am not alone in my struggles.   _yes_ _no_

Realize spiritual strength building is a long-term
process.   _yes_ _no_

Release my will to God.   _yes_ _no_

Things to Do

☐ Read the story of how God gave Samson amazing strength in Judges 13—16.

☐ Identify one or more areas in your life where you know you are weak.

☐ Ask God to give you the strength to handle struggles.

☐ Create a spiritual exercise plan consisting of prayer, fellowship with other Christians, and reading the Word to build your spiritual muscles.

☐ Share a struggle that you are experiencing with a friend and ask him or her to pray about it with you.

☐ Commit to spending time in prayer each day asking for God's strength.

☐ Read an article about someone who exhibited unusual strength in the face of adversity, such as Franklin Delano Roosevelt or Martin Luther.

Things to Remember

I will love You, O LORD, my strength.
The LORD is my rock and my fortress and
my deliverer; my God, my strength, in
whom I will trust.

PSALM 18:1–2 NKJV

It is God who arms me with strength,
and makes my way perfect. . . . For You
have armed me with strength for the
battle; You have subdued under me
those who rose up against me.

PSALM 18:32, 39 NKJV

The LORD is my light and my salvation;
whom shall I fear? The LORD is the
strength of my life; of whom shall
I be afraid?

PSALM 27:1 NKJV

The Lord is my strength and my shield;
my heart trusted in Him, and I am
helped; therefore my heart greatly
rejoices, and with my song I will
praise Him.

PSALM 28:7 NKJV

God has come to save me. I will trust in
him and not be afraid. The LORD GOD is
my strength and my song; he has
become my salvation.

ISAIAH 12:2 NLT

**The way to grow
strong in Christ is
to become weak in
yourself.**

—C. H. SPURGEON

**The acknowledgment
of our weakness
is the first step in
repairing our loss.**

—THOMAS À KEMPIS

Victory

Your Name Is on a Trophy

Thanks be to God, who gives us the victory through our Lord Jesus Christ.

—1 CORINTHIANS 15:57 NKJV

God is always victorious. Nothing is too difficult for Him. And what's more, with His help, you can be victorious too. He can lead you through to victory over any problem, issue, or struggle in your life.

While this may be easy to accept on the surface, it can be much more difficult to believe when you are in the midst of a really difficult situation. Perhaps you have a mountain of debt and wonder how you will ever be able to get out from under it. Or you may be ill or struggling with the illness of a loved one or friend. Do you feel like giving up under the pressure? Is there a difficult person in your life? Are you dealing with problems in your marriage? in your work? with your children? It's easy to become discouraged. But God wants you to lean on Him and let Him show you how to be a winner in every situation you encounter.

In the Bible, David found himself in the midst of just such a daunting challenge when he went up against a giant named Goliath. Goliath was a nine-foot-tall champion fighter who wore 125 pounds of armor and wielded a 15-pound javelin. David was a scrawny shepherd boy who probably wore goatskins and carried a slingshot. For all intents and purposes, David was completely outclassed, and Goliath should have squashed him like a bug.

However, David already knew that God had given him the victory, so when his fellow Israelites tried to dress him in heavy armor for protection, he refused it and placed his trust in God's protection. And this is what you should do when you face a seemingly impossible situation. Stop relying on your own effort and put your trust in God, for He wants you to succeed and triumph in all you do. Victory will come at a price (you'll have to work for it), and it may not come right away (you'll have to be patient), but it will come. Above all, don't focus so hard on the present problem that you miss all the other victories God gives you every day!

Step onto that battlefield just like David did and go forward with the tools God has given you—even if that means zinging a pebble at your giant. When God is in control of the situation, that little pebble will hit the problem right on the head and knock it down flat. Your feeble weapons are mighty in God's hands.

I Will

Realize that God is always victorious.   _yes_   _no_

Believe that God will give me victory.   _yes_   _no_

Remember all the little victories God gives me
each day.   _yes_   _no_

Remain confident even when I feel defeated.   _yes_   _no_

View challenges as an opportunity for victory,
not defeat.   _yes_   _no_

Believe that God is with me in my struggles.   _yes_   _no_

Trust that God will show me the way to victory.   _yes_   _no_

Things to Do

☐ *Make a list of at least five victories that God has given you
in the past year.*

☐ *Look for the little victories that God gives you each day.*

☐ *Pick out one area of your life where you have a struggle and need
victory, then give it to God in prayer.*

☐ *Read the story of David and Goliath in 1 Samuel 17.*

☐ *Talk to a friend about a failure you are experiencing and ask him to
pray about it.*

☐ *Read a story about someone who overcame great odds to win victory,
such as that of Joan of Arc (victory in battle) or Steven Hawking
(victory over physical disability).*

Things to Remember

The weapons of our warfare are not carnal but mighty in God for pulling down strongholds.

2 CORINTHIANS 10:4 NKJV

Oh, sing to the LORD a new song! For He has done marvelous things; His right hand and His holy arm have gained Him the victory.

PSALM 98:1 NKJV

Whatever is born of God overcomes the world. And this is the victory that has overcome the world—our faith.

1 JOHN 5:4 NKJV

Do you not know that those who run in a race all run, but one receives the prize? Run in such a way that you may obtain it.

1 CORINTHIANS 9:24 NKJV

Oh, clap your hands, all you peoples! Shout to God with the voice of triumph!

PSALM 47:1 NKJV

Thanks be to God who always leads us in triumph in Christ, and through us diffuses the fragrance of His knowledge in every place.

2 CORINTHIANS 2:14 NKJV

If Christ is with us, who is against us? You can fight with confidence where you are sure of victory. With Christ and for Christ victory is certain.

—SAINT BERNARD OF CLAIRVAUX

God wants us to be victors, not victims; to grow, not grovel; to soar; not sink; to overcome, not to be overwhelmed.

—WILLIAM ARTHUR WARD

Future

The Unseen Present

> "I know the plans I have for you," says the LORD. "They are plans for good and not for disaster, to give you a future and a hope."
>
> —JEREMIAH 29:11 NKJV

When you see a birthday gift on the table or a Christmas present under the tree, are you afraid to open it? Do you timidly poke at it, hoping that it won't bite you? Do you put it out on the back porch for a few days in the hopes that someone will carry it away? Of course not, because you know it's a gift that was given to you by someone who cares about you. You're excited about what that box could hold. So you dig into it—no saving the wrapping paper—and you don't stop until that gift is revealed. That's what God wants you to do with a precious gift He's given you—the future!

No matter what stage of life you are in, the future is waiting for you every morning, as new and bright as the promises of God. Don't let fear of the unknown keep you from folding back the paper and taking hold of what God has given you. Remember that He has seen the future, and He knows everything it holds for you.

Rushing out to embrace the future sounds good, but how can it not be worrisome in today's world? Television, newspapers, magazines—violent images assault us from every angle. Nothing is easy or straightforward in our high-tech, constantly changing global culture. Relationships, health issues, employment, finances, parenting—anything can happen and often does. How can a man reach out for the future in the midst of all that?

Remember this: You are the child of a loving God who knows all about you and holds your future in His hands. There is nothing you could face that He hasn't already anticipated. Spend time each day asking for His guidance and direction as you face the issues each new day brings. Choose one of the many plans for reading through the Bible in a year. This will bolster your faith and help you to glean godly principles for successful living in uncertain times. Most of all, choose faith over worry. Faith doesn't mean sticking your head in the sand. It means consciously handing off to God those things that are out of your control.

When you realize that God is always with you, the future doesn't look like such a scary place anymore. In fact, it looks more like that big Christmas gift under the tree that is just waiting to be opened. All you have to do is to trust Him and follow where He leads.

I Will

Think of the future as a gift from God.   *yes*   *no*

Believe that God is in control of my future.   *yes*   *no*

Try to live in the present, one day at a time.   *yes*   *no*

Accept that God will take care of me in the future.   *yes*   *no*

Remember what God has done for me in the past
when I start to fret about the future.   *yes*   *no*

Try to look forward to all the things God has in
store for my life.   *yes*   *no*

Realize that God will be with me all the days of
my life.   *yes*   *no*

Things to Do

☐ *Write down your worries about the future and ask God to take
care of them.*

☐ *Make a list of three to five things you would love to see happen in
your life in the next ten years.*

☐ *Think of five goals that you want to achieve in the forthcoming year.*

☐ *Memorize Revelation 22:13—"I am the Alpha and the Omega, the
Beginning and the End, the First and the Last"—and Matthew 6:27—
"Which of you by worrying can add one cubit to his stature?"*

☐ *Identify one or two situations in the past that caused you a great deal
of worry, but were not as bad in reality as they seemed to you at the
time.*

☐ *Talk to a friend and share your concerns about the future.*

Things to Remember

The path of the just is like the shining sun, that shines ever brighter unto the perfect day.

PROVERBS 4:18 NKJV

This is God, our God forever and ever; He will be our guide even to death.

PSALM 48:14 NKJV

I am persuaded that neither death nor life, nor angels nor principalities nor powers, nor things present nor things to come, nor height nor depth, nor any other created thing, shall be able to separate us from the love of God which is in Christ Jesus our Lord.

ROMANS 8:38–39 NKJV

Mark the blameless man, and observe the upright; for the future of that man is peace.

PSALM 37:37 NKJV

There is hope in your future, says the LORD.

JEREMIAH 31:17 NKJV

Let your eyes look straight ahead, and your eyelids look right before you. Ponder the path of your feet, and let all your ways be established.

PROVERBS 4:25–26 NKJV

Never be afraid to trust an unknown future to a known God.

—CORRIE TEN BOOM

His divinity is understood as the power of the future making our present appear in a new light. The future is God's: which means that, wherever an individual being goes, in life or death, God is there.

—HANS KÜNG

Prayer

Your Direct Line to God

Certainly God has heard me; He has attended to the voice of my prayer.

—Psalm 66:19 NKJV

When cell phones were introduced to the American public in 1984, people weren't quite sure what to make of these little glorified walkie-talkies. But as the technology developed over the next few years, people gradually began to realize all the benefits that cell phones could provide. You could chat with a friend while walking down the street or riding in a car, and your friends could reach you just as easily. You could contact someone with an important message, even if he or she was traveling. And cell phones could help get you out of a jam, like being stranded alongside the road or locked out of your house.

In many ways, prayer is like your direct cell-phone to God. No matter where you are or what you happen to be doing, you can simply call up God and talk to Him. And when you pray, He can speak to you just as easily. He is available twenty-four hours a day seven days a week, whether you have something very important to talk to Him about or you just want to tell

Him about your day. And when you find yourself in a jam, prayer can do much more than put you in touch with a mechanic or a locksmith—it can instantly connect you with the one who knows all things and is in control of everything that happens.

God wants to meet your needs and give you all kinds of blessings, but He also wants you to call Him up and tell Him what those needs are. It is amazing what God can do in your life when you simply ask Him! In the Bible, when Hezekiah was suffering from a grave illness and was told by the prophet Isaiah that he was going to die, he asked God to let him live a little longer. Because of his prayer, God added fifteen years to his life! When King Herod arrested Peter and was about to put him on trial, the church prayed earnestly for his release. That very night, an angel appeared and broke him out of jail. Prayer allows miracles to flow in and through your life.

But perhaps the greatest benefit of prayer is that it allows you to develop the close relationship with God that He wants to have with you. He's always listening. Through prayer you can receive His power when you are tempted to do wrong; through prayer God can instruct you on the right course of action. When you do mess up, prayer enables you to confess what you did directly to God and ask Him to forgive you. And through prayers of praise and thanksgiving to God, you can express your appreciation for everything that He has done for you. For all these reasons, the Bible tells us that we should pray continually and constantly seek fellowship with God.

With all the activities and events that go on during the day, however, it can be hard to find the time to pray. Even when you are able to set some time aside, it can sometimes be a little awkward knowing exactly what to say to God. It's important to remember that God doesn't expect you to create some special environment to pray. He just wants you to talk to Him as you would to a friend, whenever you do have a free moment.

If you're not used to praying, it might be helpful to set an initial goal of five minutes of prayer a day. Talk to God while you're alone in the car or during your evening walk. Talk to Him while you're taking your morning shower or right before you go to sleep at night. If you don't know what to say, just tell Him about your day. Share your feelings and experiences, like you would with any good friend, and don't worry about saying something profound. God just wants to hear from you.

Developing an effective prayer life is less daunting than most men realize. God doesn't even care if your prayers take the form of spoken words or inner thoughts as long as they are directed to Him. All He wants is to be there with you and for you throughout your days and nights.

Pray like this: Our Father in heaven, may your name be honored. May your Kingdom come soon. May your will be done here on earth, just as it is in heaven. Give us our food for today, and forgive us our sins, just as we have forgiven those who have sinned against us. And don't let us yield to temptation, but deliver us from the evil one.

—Matthew 6:9–13 NLT

I Will

Realize that I don't have to be perfect to talk to God. _yes_ _no_

Believe that God will listen when I pray. _yes_ _no_

Remember that God wants to meet my needs. _yes_ _no_

Allow God to speak to me in prayer. _yes_ _no_

Believe in the power of prayer. _yes_ _no_

Speak to God freely without worrying if I'm saying it right. _yes_ _no_

Trust that God will always answer my prayer. _yes_ _no_

Things to Do

☐ Read about Daniel's dedication to prayer in Daniel 6.

☐ Talk to God today while sitting in traffic or standing in line at the store or doing anything else that allows you an extra moment.

☐ Set a time to spend five minutes or more in prayer.

☐ Make a list of at least ten things to talk or ask God about.

☐ Pray with a spouse or friend about a particular need he or she has.

☐ Stick a note in your wallet, on your steering wheel, or in another place where you will see it as a reminder to pray.

☐ List two or three misconceptions that people have told you in the past about how you should pray.

Things to Remember

Jesus said, "Whatever you ask in My name, that I will do, that the Father may be glorified in the Son. If you ask anything in My name, I will do it."

JOHN 14:13–14 NKJV

Now this is the confidence that we have in Him, that if we ask anything according to His will, He hears us. And if we know that He hears us, whatever we ask, we know that we have the petitions that we have asked of Him.

1 JOHN 5:14–15 NKJV

Jesus said, "In that day you will ask Me nothing. Most assuredly, I say to you, whatever you ask the Father in My name He will give you."
—John 16:23 NKJV

O Lord, hear me praying; listen to my plea, O God my King, for I will never pray to anyone but you. Each morning I will look to you in heaven and lay my requests before you, praying earnestly.

PSALM 5:1–3 TLB

Jesus said, "When you pray, do not use vain repetitions as the heathen do. For they think that they will be heard for their many words. Therefore do not be like them. For your Father knows the things you have need of before you ask Him."

MATTHEW 6:7 NKJV

Evening and morning and at noon I will pray, and cry aloud, and He shall hear my voice.

PSALM 55:17 NKJV

Jesus said, "I say to you, love your enemies, bless those who curse you, do good to those who hate you, and pray for those who spitefully use you and persecute you."

MATTHEW 5:44 NKJV

Jesus said, "When you pray, go into your room, and when you have shut your door, pray to your Father who is in the secret place; and your Father who sees in secret will reward you openly."

MATTHEW 6:6 NKJV

Jesus said, "I say to you, whatever things you ask when you pray, believe that you receive them, and you will have them."

MARK 11:24 NKJV

The Spirit also helps in our weaknesses. For we do not know what we should pray for as we ought, but the Spirit Himself makes intercession for us with groanings which cannot be uttered.

ROMANS 8:26 NKJV

Pray without ceasing.

1 THESSALONIANS 5:17 NKJV

The more you pray, the easier it becomes. The easier it becomes, the more you will pray.

—MOTHER TERESA

Mental prayer is nothing else . . . but being on terms of friendship with God, frequently conversing in secret with Him.

—SAINT TERESA OF AVILA

Success

More than Riches and Fame

O Lord, save us; O Lord, grant us success.

—Psalm 118:25 NIV

How do you define *success*? For some people, it means having a high-paying job and the financial means to be able to afford expensive toys, like a fancy new car, a big-screen TV, and enough stereo equipment to power a rock concert. Others might say that success is having the esteem and admiration of their peers. Then still others might say they believe that success depends more on personal satisfaction and happiness in life, whether in their work, their hobbies, or their home life. In a 1997 poll conducted by California Survey Research Services, 54 percent of the respondents defined success in this way.

The problem with defining success in terms of money is that it's difficult to determine how much is enough. Will $1 million make you a success? Or will it take more like $10 million or $100 million? Does owning a Jaguar make you successful? Or does it require that you own a Jaguar and a Ferrari? Are you more successful if you have a personal home theater rather than a top-of-the-line TV and DVD Player?

If you judge success by status, to whom do you compare yourself? The Joneses down the street who are the toast of the community? Or the Smiths up the road who are leaders in their church? What if you have more education than anyone else in your workplace? Would that make you successful? Would you be inclined to consider yourself successful if you occupied the biggest office or had the longest and most important title in your company? At any given time, doesn't it seem that there is someone who is just a bit higher on the social ladder than you are?

What exactly does personal satisfaction mean to you? Should you be bouncing from one job, hobby, or relationship to the next in the ultimate pursuit of what it is that makes you truly happy? Does a successful marriage mean that you are happy and satisfied all the time?

Jesus knew that success cannot be adequately measured in these terms. He warned against storing up possessions on this earth and putting your faith in money. Fortunes are easily won and even more easily lost. If you don't think so, ask someone who made a quick fortune on tech stock and then lost it all even quicker.

Jesus also advised against using status and prestige as a measuring stick for success. He knew that public opinion is a fickle friend. Who would have imagined when Jesus rode triumphantly through the streets of Jerusalem on a bed of palm branches that one short week later the cheers would have changed to jeers and He would be crucified alongside two thieves?

So what about measuring success through personal

satisfaction? How could that be a pointless pursuit? Jesus taught His disciples that true happiness only exists in seeking God and walking in relationship with Him. In Matthew 6:33 He says, "Seek first the kingdom of God and His righteousness, and all these things shall be added to you."

God wants you to experience true and lasting success in your life. Begin by searching your heart and honestly assessing those things by which you judge your own success and that of others. Once you understand how you define your personal success, you can then let God realign your values.

To do that, you must be willing to listen carefully and follow His lead each and every day. Learn His ways by reading and studying the Bible on a regular basis. As you focus on biblical principles, God's definition of success will be established in your heart and mind.

It's also important to spend time with God in prayer, asking Him to open your eyes to His standards for success.

Remember that everything you have—wealth, charisma, talent, strength—has been given to you by God. Be sure to give Him thanks and praise for them. Be content with the gifts that He has provided for you, and use them to help others for the glory of His kingdom. As you begin to store up treasures for yourself in heaven, you will experience the true happiness that living a successful life in God can bring.

Good advice and success belong to me. Insight and strength are mine.

—Proverbs 8:14 NLT

I Will

Allow God to realign my values.   _yes_ _no_

Remember that everything comes from God.   _yes_ _no_

Look to Christ as my model for success.   _yes_ _no_

Accept the gifts that God has already given me.   _yes_ _no_

Realize that I have incredible value to God.   _yes_ _no_

Believe that I am a success.   _yes_ _no_

Serve others because I genuinely care for them and
not just to "look good."   _yes_ _no_

Things to Do

☐ Ask God to help you to rely on Him as your source of success.

☐ Compliment a friend on something you believe they are successful at.

☐ List five to ten reasons why God views you as a success.

☐ Go through a few past bank statements and put a checkmark next to anything you bought to impress others or to make yourself feel more successful.

☐ Write down two to five things that you have done in the past few weeks for the sole purpose of helping others (not for any personal recognition or gain).

☐ Look through the Gospel of Matthew and count each separate time that Jesus spoke against making wealth and status a priority before God.

Things to Remember

"My thoughts are not your thoughts, nor are your ways My ways,"
says the LORD. "For as the heavens are higher than the earth, so
are My ways higher than your ways, and My thoughts than
your thoughts."

ISAIAH 55:8–9 NKJV

Jesus said, "Sell what you have and give alms; provide yourselves
money bags which do not grow old, a treasure in the heavens
that does not fail, where no thief approaches nor moth destroys.
For where your treasure is, there your heart will be also."

LUKE 12:33–34 NKJV

We brought nothing into this world, and it is
certain we can carry nothing out. And having food
and clothing, with these we shall be content.
—1 Timothy 6:7–8 NKJV

In the Parable of the Talents, Jesus said, "His lord said to him,
'Well done, good and faithful servant; you were faithful over a
few things, I will make you ruler over many things. Enter into the
joy of your lord.'"

MATTHEW 25:21 NKJV

Keep the words of this covenant, and do them, that you may
prosper in all that you do.

DEUTERONOMY 29:9 NKJV

Hezekiah . . . did what was good and right and true before the LORD his God. And in every work that he began in the service of the house of God, in the law and in the commandment, to seek his God, he did it with all his heart. So he prospered.

2 CHRONICLES 31:20–21 NKJV

Oh, the joys of those who do not follow evil men's advice, who do not hang around with sinners, scoffing at the things of God. But they delight in doing everything God wants them to, and day and night are always meditating on his laws and thinking about ways to follow him more closely. They are like trees along a riverbank bearing luscious fruit each season without fail. Their leaves shall never wither, and all they do shall prosper.

PSALM 1:1–3 TLB

He who is of a proud heart stirs up strife, but he who trusts in the LORD will be prospered.

PROVERBS 28:25 NKJV

If the ax is dull, and one does not sharpen the edge, then he must use more strength; but wisdom brings success.

ECCLESIASTES 10:10 NKJV

It is not your business to succeed, but to do right; when you have done so, the rest lies with God.

C. S. LEWIS

A great many people go through life in bondage to success. They are in mortal dread of failure. I do not have to succeed. I have only to be true to the highest I know—success or failure are in the hands of God.

E. STANLEY JONES

Discernment

Seeing Through the Gray Matter

If any of you lacks wisdom, let him ask of God, who gives to all liberally and without reproach, and it will be given to him.

—JAMES 1:5 NKJV

The majority of situations we face in life can be labeled definitely right or definitely wrong. For example, you wouldn't consider going into a store and taking something without paying for it. That would obviously be wrong. But there are other times when the right thing to do is not quite so easy to determine. For those gray areas, we need godly discernment.

Discernment means "sound judgment." It is the ability to see through the gray and loosely defined elements of a situation and see what course of action is good and profitable and pleasing to God.

Since the earliest days of the Church, leaders have had to depend upon spiritual discernment to distinguish between those teachings that were false and those that were inspired by God. In the early church in Colosse (a region that contained a mixture of Greeks, Romans, and transplanted Jews) a number of these false teachings crept in and began to lure believers away from the teachings of the Gospel. Alarmed, one of the church leaders named Epaphras sought out Paul, who then wrote his letter to the Colossians in order to combat these false teachings.

The letters that Paul wrote to the Colossians and the other early churches provide excellent guidelines for developing discernment. In fact, Scripture should be the first place you look when confronted with a gray situation. Ask yourself these questions: Does the Bible expressly prohibit it? Does it correspond with other teachings in the Bible? Will it ultimately bring dishonor to God? Is it self-serving? Does it violate the rights of others?

If you still are unsure about the situation, talk to someone you trust and respect about the situation—perhaps your pastor. Many times, you will find that you are not the first to have struggled with a certain gray area. For that reason, the wisdom and counsel of others can be a valuable resource.

Still, the most important thing is to seek God directly and ask for His help in dealing with the issue. Ask Him to cleanse your mind of worldly compromises and generalities and clarify godly principles that apply.

God doesn't want you to be in the dark when it comes to the gray areas you encounter in life. He understands that you won't always know instantly what you are to do, but He also promises to give you the insight and discernment you need if your heart is determined to do what is right. Let Him help you as you strive to walk each day in the light.

I Will

Look to Scripture as a guide for what is
right or wrong. *yes* *no*

Seek God's wisdom for discernment. *yes* *no*

Insist on always doing what is right. *yes* *no*

Accept correction and guidance from others when
seeking discernment. *yes* *no*

Believe that God will show me the truth in
any gray area. *yes* *no*

Persist in always seeking right from wrong in any
gray situation. *yes* *no*

Things to Do

☐ *Pray specifically for wisdom to discern right from wrong in the gray areas of your life.*

☐ *Read Paul's letter to the Colossians.*

☐ *Talk to a pastor or some other person you respect about a situation in which you need discernment.*

☐ *Do some research on gnosticism (look it up in an encyclopedia or on the Web) to find out why it was such a problem in the early church.*

☐ *Look for false teachings that you receive from others throughout your day.*

☐ *Make a mini-checklist for discerning gray-area situations when they arise. Use the following questions: (1) Does the Bible expressly prohibit it? (2) Is it self-serving? (3) Does it violate my conscience?*

Things to Remember

Solid food is for the mature, who because of practice have their senses trained to discern good and evil.

HEBREWS 5:14 NASB

The word of God is living and powerful, and sharper than any two-edged sword, piercing even to the division of soul and spirit, and of joints and marrow, and is a discerner of the thoughts and intents of the heart.

HEBREWS 4:12 NKJV

This is my prayer: that your love may abound more and more in knowledge and depth of insight, so that you may be able to discern what is best and may be pure and blameless until the day of Christ.

PHILIPPIANS 1:9–10 NIV

The natural man does not receive the things of the Spirit of God, for they are foolishness to him; nor can he know them, because they are spiritually discerned. But he who is spiritual judges all things, yet he himself is rightly judged by no one.

1 CORINTHIANS 2:14–15 NKJV

The gift of discernment has been somewhat neglected in some contemporary charismatic circles, but it is perhaps the gift that most of all needs to be sought and cultivated, because its exercise is the key to the right use of all the rest.

—TOM SMAIL

God never gives us discernment in order that we may criticize, but that we may intercede.

—OSWALD CHAMBERS

Give God His Due

Give to the LORD the glory due His name; bring an offering, and come before Him. Oh, worship the LORD in the beauty of holiness!

—1 CHRONICLES 16:29 NKJV

Humans were created to worship—it's a basic instinct that dwells within every person. So strong is that inner urging, that if you don't worship God, you will seek out some other person or object to focus your affections on. The Bible refers to those other things as "idols," and they have always been a stumbling block for believers.

In the Old Testament, when Moses went up to Mount Sinai and didn't return for forty days, the Israelites melted down their jewelry and made a golden calf to worship. When God brought them into the Promised Land, they started worshiping a god called Baal.

In the New Testament, idol worship was so prevalent that Paul had to caution the Corinthian Christians not to eat food offered to them. And in 1 John 5:21, John felt compelled to write, "Little children, keep yourselves from idols."

The idols that people serve today are not images made

of metal, wood, or stone, but things like careers, activities, interests, relationships, possessions—anything that comes before God in their lives. Have you ever considered whether there may be idols in your life?

God knows that pursuing such idols can lead to feelings of emptiness. He knows the disappointment you will experience if you place your trust in them. That is why He wants you to focus your worship on Him; He will never fail you.

So check out your heart. Are there any idols on the throne of your life? Do you worship anyone or anything other than God? And remember that worship is more than saying prescribed words and expressions. It is also the devotion you show to someone or something as shown through your actions, attitudes, and priorities.

If your answer is no, you are probably already aware of the benefits of worshiping God by putting Him first in your life. If your answer is yes, it's never too late to lay aside your idols and turn your praise and worship to God alone. As you center your life on Him, you will begin to actively experience His love, and you will want to direct that love outwardly in service toward others. You will receive His wisdom and guidance to help you in everything you do, and You will receive His power and protection. Best of all, you will receive joy and fulfillment in life that only God can give.

I Will

Believe God is worthy of worship.   *yes*   *no*

Accept that if I don't worship God, I worship
other things.   *yes*   *no*

Realize the way I live my life can be a form of
worship.   *yes*   *no*

Maintain my relationship with God through worship.   *yes*   *no*

Trust that worshiping God leads to fulfillment.   *yes*   *no*

Allow God to show me the idols I have set up
in my life.   *yes*   *no*

Experience God's love through worship.   *yes*   *no*

Things to Do

- [ ] *Spend a few minutes thanking and praising God.*

- [ ] *List five to ten idols in your life that you often put before God.*

- [ ] *Write out a plan for how you will eliminate false idols in your life. Start with the phrase, "I will put God first by . . ."*

- [ ] *Read one of the following psalms of worship each morning for the next week: Psalms 8, 9, 18, 23, 66, 81, 96.*

- [ ] *Ask God to help you live a life of devotion to Him.*

- [ ] *Sing a hymn of worship in your quiet time with God.*

- [ ] *Think of one or two things that you can do for another person in the next few weeks as an act of worship to God.*

Things to Remember

Give unto the LORD the glory due to His name; worship the LORD in the beauty of holiness.

PSALM 29:2 NKJV

You must worship no other gods, but only Jehovah, for he is a God who claims absolute loyalty and exclusive devotion.

EXODUS 34:14 TLB

Jesus said, "The hour is coming, and now is, when the true worshipers will worship the Father in spirit and truth; for the Father is seeking such to worship Him. God is Spirit, and those who worship Him must worship in spirit and truth."

JOHN 4:23–24 NKJV

Oh come, let us worship and bow down; let us kneel before the LORD our Maker. For He is our God, and we are the people of His pasture, and the sheep of His hand.

PSALM 95:6–7 NKJV

Who shall not fear You, O Lord, and glorify Your name? For You alone are holy. For all nations shall come and worship before You, for Your judgments have been manifested.

REVELATION 15:4 NKJV

We may be truly said to worship God, though we lack perfection; but we cannot be said to worship Him if we lack sincerity.

—STEPHEN CHARNOCK

Worship is the highest and noblest activity of which man, by the grace of God, is capable.

—JOHN STOTT

Fellowship

Walking Together

I plead with you, brethren, by the name of our Lord Jesus Christ, that you all speak the same thing, and that there be no divisions among you, but that you be perfectly joined together in the same mind and in the same judgment.

1 CORINTHIANS 1:10 NKJV

How much do you think about the miracle that happens when you reach over, click on the lamp by your bed, and the room fills with light? You probably don't give it much thought at all. But what if one part of that lamp were missing? Without a switch, no electricity would travel to the bulb. Without a bulb, the electricity has nothing to illuminate. If there were no lampshade, the light would be blinding. If there were no stand or base, the lamp would fall over and might even burn a hole in your mattress. To work effectively and provide you with just the right amount of light, each part of the lamp must be present and operational. In the same way, light comes to the world as unique individuals come together in fellowship.

Jesus and his disciples knew the value of fellowship. When He was preparing for His ministry, Jesus chose twelve individuals to travel with Him and share in all His experiences. Twelve very different men—with different personalities, lifestyles, professions, temperaments, social status—united in love and devotion to Jesus and the heavenly Father He came to tell them about. Together, they traveled through the countryside changing lives in every place that they visited.

The early church came together in order to receive encouragement and strength during a time of persecution and severe hardship. The members were weak and vulnerable on their own, but together they were strong. Together they were able. Together they brought hope to those who were without hope. Together they ushered in the age of the Holy Spirit, demonstrating His power through miracles, and His nature through their selflessness.

The principle of fellowship is one that still works today. As you come together with other believers, you help to bring the light of God's love to those around you. So don't try to be a lone ranger. That only diminishes the influence your life can have in the world. Make an effort to come together with others in true godly fellowship. That will require you to make a commitment—not only to God, but also to other believers. You must be committed to spending time together, to listening to one another, to working together for the common good. It requires a commitment to lay aside petty disagreements and let God use you to help bring light to a darkened world.

I Will

Value fellowship in my life.   *yes*   *no*

Believe that God wants fellowship with me.   *yes*   *no*

Insist on never letting a busy schedule get in the
way of fellowship.   *yes*   *no*

Accept that I need camaraderie with others.   *yes*   *no*

Remember fellowship when I need strength and
support.   *yes*   *no*

Realize even friction in fellowship can be beneficial
at times.   *yes*   *no*

View fellowship as a priority in my life.   *yes*   *no*

Things to Do

☐ *Ask God to bring new friends into your life for fellowship.*

☐ *Plan to meet with friends and have fellowship in the next week.*

☐ *Read Acts 2 about the importance of fellowship in the early church.*

☐ *Spend some time in fellowship with God.*

☐ *Get to know an acquaintance better by inviting him or her to your
home for dinner or just to hang out.*

☐ *Memorize Matthew 18:20—"Where two or three are gathered together
in My name, I am there in the midst of them."*

Things to Remember

Let us consider one another in order to stir up love and good works, not forsaking the assembling of ourselves together, as is the manner of some, but exhorting one another, and so much the more as you see the Day approaching.

HEBREWS 10:24–25 NKJV

They continued steadfastly in the apostles' doctrine and fellowship, in the breaking of bread, and in prayers.

ACTS 2:42 NKJV

Two are better than one, because they have a good reward for their labor.

ECCLESIASTES 4:9 NKJV

If we walk in the light as He is in the light, we have fellowship with one another, and the blood of Jesus Christ His Son cleanses us from all sin.

1 JOHN 1:7 NKJV

God composed the body, having given greater honor to that part which lacks it, that there should be no schism in the body, but that the members should have the same care for one another. And if one member suffers, all the members suffer with it; or if one member is honored, all the members rejoice with it.

1 CORINTHIANS 12:24–26 NKJV

Behind every saint stands another saint.

—FRIEDRICH VON HÜGEL

God calls us not to solitary sainthood but to fellowship in a company of committed men.

—DAVID SCHULLER

Spiritual Growth Spurts

Grow in the grace and knowledge of our Lord and Savior Jesus Christ.

—2 PETER 3:18 NKJV

Think back. As a young teenager, do you remember a period of time when it seemed like you had to have new clothes every few weeks? You barely got them home from the store before you noticed your pants were hitting the high-water level and you had more arm than shirtsleeve. You might also remember your parents' distress as they calculated the cost of keeping you appropriately dressed. This phenomenon, common to the male gender, is referred to as a growth spurt. During this period of intense growth, boys can gain as much as four inches in height in one year.

These growth spurts are often problematic. Limbs can develop at different rates and leave a teenager feeling awkward and clumsy. They can also be painful. The layers of soft cartilage from which bones grow can be aggravated by the stress of activities such as running or jumping. Once the bones harden, the pain eases up, but until that happens they can be difficult to deal with. Growth spurts are no fun, but they are necessary if the adolescent body is to grow and mature into adulthood.

Spiritual growth spurts can be equally as uncomfortable. When you are growing as a Christian, you may find yourself feeling uncomfortable, especially in situations of immaturity that caused you no difficulty in the past. You may also discover yourself feeling clumsy and uncoordinated when talking to mature Christians who seem to have more profound insights than you and are able to back up their statements with Scripture. You may even find yourself challenging the accuracy of some of the ideas you learned from your parents and teachers. This is always an unsettling feeling.

While disconcerting, these spiritual growth spurts are just as necessary to maturity as their physical counterparts—maturity in Christ, that is. Consider the apostle Peter, who left his life as a fisherman to follow Jesus. At first, he found himself confused by Jesus' parables and had to ask Him what they meant. There were times when Jesus put Peter in uncomfortable situations by asking him challenging questions. But those must have seemed like small potatoes compared to the times that Jesus tested Peter's faith—like when He told him to get out of the boat and walk on the water. Undoubtedly, those spiritual growth spurts were challenging. But they played an important part in Peter's development as a great leader.

Of course, spiritual growth is not exactly like physical growth. Physical growth will occur whether you want it to or not—all you have to do is eat enough to meet your body's growing needs. Spiritual growth, on the other hand, requires effort and determination. While God will sometimes put you in situations to test your faith and make you grow spiritually, you will still have to work to grow in the grace and knowledge of Jesus Christ.

The initial step to stimulating spiritual growth in your life is through careful study of the Word of God. Read a chapter or two from the Bible each day. As you read, you will find that spiritual principles and insights will begin to become clear to you.

The second step is to take those revelations with you to prayer and ask God to show you how to apply them to your everyday life. Prayer is essential. It is the soul food that fuels your spiritual growth.

Eventually, these efforts will culminate in what Paul referred to as the renewal of your mind, a process by which God transforms you from your old childish self into a new creation in Christ. Like Peter, who was transformed from a clueless fisherman into the man who led more than three thousand people to Christ in one day, God will help you grow in wisdom and character until you are ready to fulfill His plan and purpose for your life.

Grow in the grace and knowledge of our Lord and Savior Jesus Christ. To Him be the glory both now and forever.

—2 Peter 3:18 NKJV

I Will

Accept the fact that spiritual growth may be
uncomfortable at times.

yes   *no*

Allow God to show me ways to grow spiritually.

yes   *no*

Believe that God wants me to grow in Him.

yes   *no*

Trust that God will be with me through painful
periods of growth.

yes   *no*

Determine to work toward Christian maturity
in my life.

yes   *no*

Remind myself that like Peter, God can transform me
into a great leader for Him and for the church.

yes   *no*

Things to Do

☐ *On paper, list a few situations in your life that have helped you grow
spiritually.*

☐ *Read some of Peter's growth experiences in Luke 5:1–11; Matthew
14:22–36; Luke 9:18–27; Luke 22:24–38; Luke 22:54–62; John
21:1–19; and Acts 2:14–41.*

☐ *Spend five minutes in prayer tomorrow morning asking God to provide
situations in your life that will help you grow spiritually.*

☐ *For twenty-one days, read a different chapter from one of the books of
the New Testament.*

☐ *List three spiritual goals for the coming year.*

☐ *Identify some of the ways that you have acted spiritually like a child in
the past, and then identify how you will change this behavior in the
future.*

Things to Remember

The godly shall flourish like palm trees and grow tall as the cedars of Lebanon. For they are transplanted into the Lord's own garden and are under his personal care. Even in old age they will still produce fruit and be vital and green.

PSALM 92:12–14 TLB

No prolonged infancies among us, please. We'll not tolerate babes in the woods, small children who are an easy mark for impostors. God wants us to grow up, to know the whole truth and tell it in love—like Christ in everything.

EPHESIANS 4:15 THE MESSAGE

Put off, concerning your former conduct, the old man which grows corrupt according to the deceitful lusts, and be renewed in the spirit of your mind.
—Ephesians 4:22–23 NKJV

Christ gives the body its strength, and he uses its joints and muscles to hold it together, as it grows by the power of God.

COLOSSIANS 2:19 CEV

We are bound to thank God always for you, brethren, as it is fitting, because your faith grows exceedingly, and the love of every one of you all abounds toward each other.

2 THESSALONIANS 1:3 NKJV

As newborn babes, desire the pure milk of the word, that you may grow thereby.

1 PETER 2:2 NKJV

I'm an olive tree, growing green in God's
house.

PSALM 52:8 THE MESSAGE

Like an open book, you watched me
grow from conception to birth; all the
stages of my life were spread out before
you.

PSALM 139:16 THE MESSAGE

Grow a wise heart—you'll do yourself a
favor; keep a clear head—you'll find a
good life.

PROVERBS 19:8 THE MESSAGE

Jesus said, "In a word, what I'm saying
is, Grow up. You're kingdom subjects.
Now live like it. Live out your God-
created identity."

MATTHEW 5:48 THE MESSAGE

Jesus said, "If you grow a healthy tree,
you'll pick healthy fruit. If you grow a
diseased tree, you'll pick worm-eaten
fruit. The fruit tells you about the tree."

MATTHEW 12:33 THE MESSAGE

Paul wrote: I long to visit you so I can
share a spiritual blessing with you that
will help you grow strong in the Lord.

ROMANS 1:11 NLT

**Growing spiritually
can be like a roller
coaster ride. Take
comfort in the
knowledge that the
way down is only
preparation for the
way up.**

—REBBE NACHMAN

**Little things come
daily, hourly within
our reach, and they
are not less
calculated to set
forward our growth
in holiness than
are the greater
occasions, which
occur but rarely.**

—JEAN-NICOLAS GROU

Friendship

A Man's Best Friend Is His Friend

There are "friends" who pretend to be friends, but there is a friend who sticks closer than a brother.

When you were a little boy, do you remember how important your best friend was to you? The first thing you wanted to do the minute you woke up every morning was run to his house so you could play. And that was the last place you were before your mom called you home for bedtime.

Your friendships today can be as great as they have ever been. They may not develop as easily or be as easy to maintain as in the past, but the effort will be more than worth it. The one thing that will help you be a better friend and enjoy deeper friendships is to realize that you can have (and you need) a variety of friendships because everyone brings something different to each relationship.

Some friendships are casual, in which you may hang out once in a while to just kick back and watch a game or a race on the tube. In these relationships the most serious conversation you ever delve into might be whether to get buffalo wings with hot or mild sauce. But that is OK. Trying to make these friendships into something more might ruin what you have—a level of comfort and lightheartedness not found in other friendships.

Another kind of friendship may be a mentoring relationship, in which a person can offer wisdom, experience, and motivation to the other. One may need spiritual guidance, while another needs help with his career. One may want to better manage his finances, while another seeks to become a better handyman around the house and garage. In such a friendship, you gain valuable information and skills while building a lasting relationship.

A third type of friendship, the deepest kind possible, is not experienced too often by men. Men may fear too much about how the relationship might appear to others. In 1 Samuel 20, you can read about Jonathan and David, who loved each other. That's supposed to be comforting, but instead it may freak some men out. Jonathan and David were allies, though, teamed up in a life-or-death situation. What cause or battle can you face together with your friend? Find that and your friendship will deepen and be envied by others.

Don't be discouraged when you first try to deepen existing or develop new friendships, because they don't always come easy. Just like a tall, strong, mature tree, your friendships need to develop healthy roots if they are going to not only survive but flourish. Make an effort to open up a little more. Be genuine and forthcoming, and soon you'll see your friendships transform and grow.

I Will

Never settle for having numerous acquaintances but
no deep friendships.   _yes_   _no_

Be willing to share meaningful things from my life
with my closest friends.   _yes_   _no_

Learn not to expect my friendships to be perfect.   _yes_   _no_

Let God show me how I can be a better friend.   _yes_   _no_

Never let miles, schedules, or other obstacles keep
me from being a true friend.   _yes_   _no_

Always strive to value my friends as I did when I was
a child.   _yes_   _no_

Things to Do

☐ *Ask God to help you be more loyal and giving.*

☐ *Drop a note via e-mail or snail mail to let a friend know how much you value him and his friendship.*

☐ *Ask a friend if he needs help working around the yard or in the garage—before he asks for it.*

☐ *Ask for (and remember) the birth dates for your friend and his family, as well as his and his wife's wedding anniversary. Send cards annually to let him know that he is on your mind.*

☐ *Read the Gospel of John to find out how Jesus was the ultimate friend to his disciples.*

☐ *Let friends know firsthand important news about yourself—before they hear it from anyone else.*

Things to Remember

Friends love through all kinds of weather, and families stick together in all kinds of trouble.

PROVERBS 17:17 THE MESSAGE

The Scripture was fulfilled which says, "Abraham believed God, and it was accounted to him for righteousness." And he was called the friend of God.

JAMES 2:23 NKJV

Faithful are the wounds of a friend, but the kisses of an enemy are deceitful.

PROVERBS 27:6 NKJV

Just as iron sharpens iron, friends sharpen the minds of each other.

—PROVERBS 27:17 CEV

In all my prayers for all of you, I always pray with joy because of your partnership in the gospel from the first day until now.

PHILIPPIANS 1:4–5 NIV

If they fall, one will lift up his companion. But woe to him who is alone when he falls, for he has no one to help him up.

ECCLESIASTES 4:10 NKJV

So long as we love we serve; so long as we are loved by others, I would almost say that we are indispensable; and no man is useless while he has a friend.

—ROBERT LOUIS STEVENSON

Think where man's glory most begins and ends, and say my glory was I had such friends.

—WILLIAM BUTLER YEATS

God's Word

God's Road Map and Journal All in One

Your word is a lamp to my feet and a light to my path.

—PSALM 119:105 NKJV

When you consider that the Bible was written in three different languages over a period of fifteen hundred years by more than forty different authors, the fact that it remains thematically consistent from beginning to end is truly remarkable. But what is even more remarkable is that people still find the Bible as applicable to their lives today as when it was first written thousands of years ago.

The reason? The Bible doesn't just quote long and complicated rules for living. Instead, it shows readers through stories and examples what happens when they choose to follow or to disobey those rules. Since the struggles that the characters in the Bible deal with are typically similar to the ones people experience today, readers can relate to them and learn how that biblical person handled or failed to handle a situation.

Suppose you are facing an overwhelming challenge in your life. Turning to Proverbs 3:5, you read: "Trust in the

Lord with all your heart, and lean not on your own understanding." Sounds great, but how do you put this into practice in your own life? Flipping forward to Matthew 14, you discover the story of Peter, who trusted Christ enough to step over the side of the boat and actually begin to walk across the water. However, the moment he began to trust in his own understanding, he lost faith and started to sink.

Of course, to apply the Bible to your life, you first have to read and comprehend what it is saying. Start by reading enough of the story to get an idea of the context in which it is set. Don't just read one verse here and there, but tackle a whole chapter at a time. Use a Bible handbook or study Bible to find out what the passage meant to the people at the time it was written. Now you're ready to determine what it means to you in your current situation.

Not only is the Bible God's road map to keep you from losing your way in life, but it is also a personal journal of the people whose stories are recorded in it. Through the experiences and struggles of these people, God will give you the wisdom to solve problems, the ability to distinguish right from wrong, and the inspiration to follow the examples of those who obeyed Him. So don't miss out! Read the Bible— God's road map and journal all in one.

I Will

Allow God to provide guidance for my life through the reading of His Word.

yes   _no_

Accept my failings as draw strength from the characters I read about in the Bible.

yes   _no_

Let God speak to me through His Word.

yes   _no_

Exhibit the promises in God's Word in my life.

yes   _no_

Appreciate the Bible and view it as a gift from God.

yes   _no_

Always look for the practical application of biblical stories in my life.

yes   _no_

Things to Do

☐ _Ask God to give you understanding as you read the Bible._

☐ _Write a paragraph comparing a situation that you have recently experienced to one that a character in the Bible experienced (for example, you may have been in a situation like Peter where you had trouble trusting God)._

☐ _Read some the stories of the "founding fathers" of Israel: Abraham in Genesis 15, 18, and 22; Jacob in Genesis 27, 28:10–22, 32–33; and Joseph in Genesis 37, 39—45._

☐ _Read the story of Jesus' early ministry on earth in Mark 1—6._

☐ _Schedule time each day for the next two weeks to read five to six chapters out of a book in the Bible._

☐ _Memorize Psalm 119:105—"Your word is a lamp to my feet and a light to my path."_

Things to Remember

More to be desired are they than gold, yea, than much fine gold; sweeter also than honey and the honeycomb. Moreover by them Your servant is warned, and in keeping them there is great reward.

PSALM 19:10–11 NKJV

All Scripture is given by inspiration of God, and is profitable for doctrine, for reproof, for correction, for instruction in righteousness.

2 TIMOTHY 3:16 NKJV

Jesus said, "The words that I speak to you are spirit, and they are life."

JOHN 6:63 NKJV

Concerning the works of men, by the word of Your lips, I have kept away from the paths of the destroyer.

PSALM 17:4 NKJV

How can a young man cleanse his way? By taking heed according to Your word. . . . Your word I have hidden in my heart, that I might not sin against You.

PSALM 119:9, 11 NKJV

Every word of God is pure; He is a shield to those who put their trust in Him.

PROVERBS 30:5 NKJV

All the knowledge you want is comprised in one book, the Bible.

—JOHN WESLEY

The Bible is a book of faith, and a book of doctrine, and a book of morals, and a book of religion, of special revelation from God, but it is also a book which teaches man his own individual responsibility, his own dignity, and his equity with his fellow-man.

—DANIEL WEBSTER

Goals

Aim, Shoot, Score

I press toward the goal for the prize of the upward call of God in Christ Jesus.

—Philippians 3:14 NKJV

The pursuit of goals is a great American pastime. Few people make it through childhood and adolescence without numerous attempts by parents, teachers, coaches, and other caring adults to instill the principle that setting and reaching goals is the key to success in life. It is the way to become a better student, a better athlete, and an overall better person, you have been reminded again and again. You have heard the often-used admonition that goes "If you aim at nothing, you'll probably hit it."

Goals certainly are important. They give direction and purpose to your life. They are the building blocks to your dreams. Nevertheless, many people drift through life, hoping for little and accomplishing less because they never have learned how to set appropriate and productive goals. They find goal-setting difficult because they haven't determined what is really important to them—what standard of success they wish to reach.

This culture generally defines a successful life as one marked by knowledge, wealth, status, or celebrity. Even in the Christian community those criteria are touted. A church is successful if it has a large, expensive facility, a membership list in the thousands, activities for every day of the week, and lots of notoriety. These standards are neither good nor bad. But they are insignificant when compared with the standard for success set by the apostle Paul in the verse quoted above.

Paul's standard of success was the "prize of the upward call of God in Christ Jesus." And he set his goals accordingly. He was determined to become all that God intended him to be. What is your standard of success? What goals have you set in your pursuit of that standard?

If your standard of success is to win the prize for which God has called you—God's perfect will and purpose for your life—then your goals must be first and foremost established in prayer. The apostle Paul spent a lot of time on his knees, and you will have to do the same if you are to set goals that will take you where you want to go. Pouring out your heart to God will help you see who you truly are and rightly evaluate your motives and desires. Then listening to God—the second part of prayer—will help you refine those motives and desires in light of God's will and purpose.

Once you've set some goals, it's time to create a clearly defined course of action for how you will achieve each one. Again, prayer is important. Ask God to show you where you need to make corrections or where you need to be flexible going forward. Each goal should have its own list of specific steps. And don't forget to put it all in writing.

Next, choose one or two people who will agree to review your goals and pray with you as you set out on your journey of accomplishment. Select individuals who have already achieved goals similar to your own in their lives. Keep in mind that this should not be a one-meeting commitment. Get together often to share your progress and ask for advice. Ask if you can make yourself accountable to them as you go through your action steps.

The last step is to celebrate the achievement of each and every goal. It doesn't matter if that goal was to obtain a college degree or to take one course at the community college, to save up for a big purchase or to meet a sales goal for your company. It doesn't matter if your goal was big and intimidating or small and doable. When you have triumphed, stop and congratulate yourself and those who have helped you along the way. Send your helpers a note of thanks and pause to thank God—formally and specifically—for helping you do what you set out to do.

No matter what course you feel compelled to take in life, goals are a positive way to help you navigate your way to success. Goals that are anchored in the bedrock of prayer and godly wisdom will surely put you on the road to fulfillment. So set your goals high in your quest for the prize of heaven—a life of fellowship with God and obedience to His will, a life of true success.

Our only power and success come from God.

—2 Corinthians 3:5 NLT

I Will

Realize the value and importance of having
goals in my life.

yes _____ *no* _____

Allow God to prioritize my goals.

yes _____ *no* _____

Believe that God will reveal the goals He
wants me to have.

yes _____ *no* _____

Accept God's correction when I set the wrong goals.

yes _____ *no* _____

Try to relax and not let my goals take over my life.

yes _____ *no* _____

Trust that God will help me achieve my goals.

yes _____ *no* _____

Things to Do

☐ *Read Paul's entire discourse on setting the right goals in Philippians 3:1–21.*

☐ *List a few of the wrong goals that you have pursued in the past.*

☐ *Ask God what goals He would like for you to pursue. Write them down.*

☐ *Go over the goals you've written down and write out your thoughts on each one—potential benefits, potential obstacles.*

☐ *Set a time to meet with a friend within the next month to talk about your goals.*

☐ *Write down a clearly defined course of action for how you will achieve each goal.*

☐ *Ask two friends or family members to pray for you as you attempt to achieve your goals.*

Things to Remember

Write the vision and make it plain on tablets, that he may run who reads it. For the vision is yet for an appointed time; but at the end it will speak, and it will not lie. Though it tarries, wait for it; because it will surely come, it will not tarry.

HABAKKUK 2:2–3 NKJV

Let us fix our eyes on Jesus, the author and perfecter of our faith, who for the joy set before him endured the cross, scorning its shame, and sat down at the right hand of the throne of God.

HEBREWS 12:2 NIV

We make it our aim . . . to be well pleasing to Him.
—2 Corinthians 5:9 NKJV

I don't mean to say that I have already achieved these things or that I have already reached perfection! But I keep working toward that day when I will finally be all that Christ Jesus saved me for and wants me to be.

PHILIPPIANS 3:12 NLT

Have two goals: wisdom—that is, knowing and doing right—and common sense. Don't let them slip away, for they fill you with living energy and bring you honor and respect.

PROVERBS 3:21–22 TLB

Wisdom is the main pursuit of sensible men, but a fool's goals are at the ends of the earth!

PROVERBS 17:24 TLB

All athletes practice strict self-control. They do it to win a prize that will fade away, but we do it for an eternal prize.

1 CORINTHIANS 9:25 NLT

Our goal is to measure up to God's plan for us.

2 CORINTHIANS 10:13 TLB

What I once thought was valuable is worthless. Nothing is as wonderful as knowing Christ Jesus my Lord. I have given up everything else and count it all as garbage. All I want is Christ.

PHILIPPIANS 3:7–8 CEV

Jesus said, "I'm praying not only for them but also for those who will believe in me. . . . The goal is for all of them to become one heart and mind—just as you, Father, are in me and I in you."

JOHN 17:20–21 THE MESSAGE

For as long, then, as that promise of resting in him pulls us on to God's goal for us, we need to be careful that we're not disqualified.

HEBREWS 4:1 THE MESSAGE

The poorest of all men is not the one without gold, but without a goal. Life for him has no meaning—no reason for living.

—AUTHOR UNKNOWN

Setting a goal is not the main thing. It is deciding how you will go about achieving it and staying with the plan.

—TOM LANDRY

God's Forgiveness

The Marvelous Gift of Forgiveness

Blessed is he whose transgression is forgiven,
whose sin is covered.

—Psalm 32:1 NKJV

Gift-giving and getting can be a tricky business. Haven't you received gifts that just didn't suit you at all? Stuff like a baggy sweater that reaches halfway to your kneecaps, a pink polo shirt, pots and pans (you don't cook), a plaid sport coat, another set of nail clippers, the list could go on forever. It's easy to see that the giver meant well, but . . . you probably had those gifts packed up and ready to return to the store by sundown.

You have been given one gift, however, that you'd never want to throw away, give away, or return to the store. That is the gift of God's forgiveness. This marvelous gift has the power to free you from the torment that guilt and regret bring to your life. It can help you put the past behind you and open your eyes to the bright future you have before you. It can renew your sense of worth and restore you to fellowship with God and with others.

The English poet Alexander Pope once said, "To err is

human, to forgive divine." This pretty much sums up the human condition—we all make mistakes and need God's divine forgiveness in our lives. That's why forgiveness is such an incredible gift. When you are truly sorry for the wrongs you have done, He forgives you and wipes the slate clean. In His eyes, it is like your wrongs never happened.

Are you struggling with sin that you feel is too big for God to forgive? Remember that no sin is unforgivable in God's eyes. There may be consequences to deal with in this life—broken relationships that can't be mended, broken laws that require a penalty, borrowed money that must be repaid. But God will be there to help you see your way through the consequences if you place your trust in Him.

Maybe you think your sin is too small for God to notice. Do you imagine that little white lies and careless indiscretions will take care of themselves? They may not have great consequences in this life, but left unforgiven, they will obstruct your fellowship with a holy and just God.

Whether your sins are big or small, they need to be plunged into the sea of God's forgiveness. Until they are, you will be unable to live a life filled with peace. You will be unable to fulfill the wonderful plans God has for you.

How do you obtain this gift of forgiveness? That part is simple. All you do is ask for it. Ask God to wash you clean with the precious blood of Jesus. Confess each sinful thought and act. Ask with a humble, repentant heart.

Perhaps the American writer Mark Twain summed it up best. He said, "Forgiveness is the fragrance that the violet sheds on the heel that has crushed it." It is an awesome gift from God that you'd never want to return.

I Will

Allow God to show me the areas in my life where I
need forgiveness.

yes *no*

Trust God's promise that He will forgive me.

yes *no*

Freely accept God's gift of forgiveness and not try to
earn it.

yes *no*

Exhibit God's forgiveness in my life by sharing it
with others.

yes *no*

Let God show me how to forgive myself.

yes *no*

Believe that others will forgive me when I've done
something to hurt them.

yes *no*

Things to Do

☐ *Write out a prayer thanking God for His free gift of forgiveness.*

☐ *Make a list of some of the wrong things you have done in the past.
Accept God's forgiveness, then cross each one off the list.*

☐ *Read how Jesus freely offered forgiveness in Matthew 9:1–8 and Luke
7:36–50.*

☐ *Tell someone about the best gift you ever received and how it made
you feel.*

☐ *Make a list of the people you need to forgive and pray over the names,
asking God to help you release them without holding a grudge.*

☐ *Memorize Jesus' words on how often you should forgive in Matthew
18:22. "Jesus said to him, 'I do not say to you, up to seven times, but
up to seventy times seven.'" Write a paragraph about what the gift of
forgiveness means to you.*

Things to Remember

"Come now, and let us reason together," says the LORD. "Though your sins are like scarlet, they shall be as white as snow; though they are red like crimson, they shall be as wool."

ISAIAH 1:18 NKJV

You, being dead in your trespasses and the uncircumcision of your flesh, He has made alive together with Him, having forgiven you all trespasses.

COLOSSIANS 2:13 NKJV

If we confess our sins, He is faithful and just to forgive us our sins and to cleanse us from all unrighteousness.

1 JOHN 1:9 NKJV

As far as the east is from the west, so far has He removed our transgressions from us.

PSALM 103:12 NKJV

Let it be known to you, brethren, that through this Man is preached to you the forgiveness of sins; and by Him everyone who believes is justified from all things from which you could not be justified by the law of Moses.

ACTS 13:38–39 NKJV

The symbol of the religion of Jesus is the cross, not the scales.

—JOHN STOTT

There is only one person God cannot forgive. The person who refuses to come to him for forgiveness.

—AUTHOR UNKNOWN

Honesty

The Only Policy

"In your anger do not sin!" Do not let the sun go down while you are still angry.

—EPHESIANS 4:26 NIV

Honesty, integrity, sincerity. These words roll easily off your tongue. What do they really mean? How are they measured? Some believe that honest means strict conformity to a set of rules and regulations. Others feel that God had something more in mind—a personal policy of honesty that extends beyond the letter of the law to the spirit behind it. Rather than being constrained to be honest from without, God wants His followers to conform to a spirit of honest that comes from within.

Making honesty your policy isn't an easy task. It means choosing to be honest, forthright, and sincere in every situation. It can be pretty tempting to shade the truth when a friend points out that you've made a mistake or when someone you love asks you a tough question and you know the answer will make the questioner unhappy. Being honest can feel pretty uncomfortable at the time, but over the long haul, your commitment to the truth will build others' trust in you and strengthen your personal and professional relationships.

God wants to turn you away from dishonesty because He knows the harm that lies and deception can cause. He understands that little lies have a habit of becoming big complications that can steal your joy and fill you with guilt, pain, and anxiety.

Honesty, on the other hand, will keep you rightly aligned with God and others. It will open your heart and mind to positive change and free you to be yourself—the unique individual that God created you to be.

Do yourself and those around you a favor. Determine each day to be truthful in every situation, no matter how tempting it might be to do otherwise. Decide also to be responsible when you share the truth with another person. Remember that the truth can hurt, even if it is something that the person needs to hear. Be sensitive to the person's feelings and ask God to give you the right words.

It is important to remember that no one is perfect. As you strive to live an honest life, you will have setbacks and disappointments. It's best to ask God for forgiveness whenever you fail to be totally truthful and then to go on, making an effort to shore up the weak points with prayer and God's Word. Most important, don't give up or become discouraged. God wants you to experience the benefits of making honesty the only policy for your life.

I Will

Determine to always tell others the truth in a
loving manner.

yes   _no_

Humble myself and determine to accept fault
for my mistakes.

yes   _no_

Confess my dishonesty to God whenever I fail
in my quest for honesty.

yes   _no_

Allow God to point out and help me correct
dishonest motives and mind-sets.

yes   _no_

Be watchful of situations where I am tempted to lie.

yes   _no_

Strive to build trust in others through living an
honest life.

yes   _no_

Things to Do

☐ *Mentally review a recent situation where you were completely honest with someone. Write down the insights you learned from that situation.*

☐ *For three days, keep track of the number of times each day that you were faced with an honesty issue.*

☐ *Read Paul's comments about living an honest life in Ephesians 4:17— 5:21.*

☐ *Compliment a friend or coworker on something you honestly believe that person does well.*

☐ *Get a copy of your company's code of ethics or policy sheet and write on it: Personal Policy: I will strive to be honest in every situation.*

☐ *List three to four situations in the past month where you have not acted honestly. Write out an action plan for how you will act honestly in the future when similar situations arise.*

Things to Remember

Paul wrote: I always try to maintain a clear conscience before God and everyone else.

ACTS 24:16 NLT

No one believes a liar, but everyone respects the words of an honest man.

PROVERBS 21:28 TLB

Honest people speak sensibly, but deceitful liars will be silenced.

PROVERBS 10:31 CEV

Truthful witness by a good person clears the air, but liars lay down a smoke screen of deceit.

PROVERBS 12:17 THE MESSAGE

The Lord hates cheating and delights in honesty.

PROVERBS 11:1 TLB

A good man's mind is filled with honest thoughts; an evil man's mind is crammed with lies.

PROVERBS 12:5 TLB

We can say with confidence and a clear conscience that we have been honest and sincere in all our dealings.

2 CORINTHIANS 1:12 NLT

I hope I shall possess firmness and virtue enough to maintain what I consider the most enviable of all titles, the character of an honest man.

—GEORGE WASHINGTON

Honesty has a beautiful and refreshing simplicity about it. No ulterior motives. No hidden meanings.

—CHARLES R. SWINDOLL

Hope

Beyond the Open Door

Lord, what do I wait for? My hope is in you.

—PSALM 39:7 NKJV

Hope is a wonderful thing—a life-giving thing. Hope is why children look for a gift under the Christmas tree even when times are hard and finances are tight. Hope makes people reach out for the joys of life.

When you place your hope in Christ, it means that you are looking forward with anticipation to the things that God has promised, and that you expect those promises to be fulfilled. When you read God's promise in John 3:16 that whoever believes in Him will be given eternal life, you believe in your heart it is true, even though you can't directly confirm it, and you expect it will be given to you. When you read a little later in John 10:10 that God has given you life abundantly, you hope—meaning you desire and expect—that this will come to pass.

Imagine yourself in a room that has hundreds of

doors. You look around and wonder which one you should try to go through. You ask God to show you, and immediately one opens. Through faith, you believe God has opened that door for you. Through hope, you expect God to lead you beyond that open door into a new and wonderful place.

When you place your hope in God, your outlook on life changes. You begin to believe that the impossible can occur even if the facts say otherwise, for with God all things are possible. You can look to the future and honestly believe a better day is coming, even in the worst situations. When Paul was imprisoned, his hope in Christ made him anticipate the future, regardless of what its outcome might be. If he lived, he looked forward to continuing his ministry with the people in the churches he had nurtured. If he died, he knew he would be with Christ, which was better by far!

Hope in God will revive you and make you want to experience life to its fullest. It will support you through the tough times and calm your anxieties. So ask God to fill you with His hope. Believe in the promises of God that you read in the Bible, and rejoice in the fact that He will always fulfill them. God has opened the door for your life—He wants you to step through it and experience what lies beyond.

I Will

Allow God to fill me with His hope.   *yes*   *no*

Trust that God will give me hope for the future.   *yes*   *no*

Exhibit the hope that I have discovered in
Christ to others.   *yes*   *no*

Remember God's promises when things look bleak.   *yes*   *no*

Honestly believe that genuine change in my life can
always occur when God is in charge.   *yes*   *no*

Accept the fact that I don't always know what will
happen in the future, but that God always does.   *yes*   *no*

Remind myself to look for the doors that God opens
for me in my life.   *yes*   *no*

Things to Do

☐ *List a few things about yourself that you would like to change, but
have given up hoping will ever change.*

☐ *Share a few of your hopes and frustrations with a friend.*

☐ *Write out a prayer asking God to fill you with hope for the future.*

☐ *Memorize John 10:10—"I have come that they may have life,
and that they may have it more abundantly."*

☐ *Stick a note on your bathroom mirror to remind you to face each new
day with hope.*

☐ *Make a list of at least four things that you hope will happen
in the future.*

Things to Remember

Remember the word to Your servant, upon which You have caused me to hope.

PSALM 119:49 NKJV

If in this life only we have hope in Christ, we are of all men the most pitiable. But now Christ is risen from the dead.

1 CORINTHIANS 15:19–20 NKJV

This certain hope of being saved is a strong and trustworthy anchor for our souls, connecting us with God himself behind the sacred curtains of heaven.

HEBREWS 6:19 TLB

I have set the LORD always before me; because He is at my right hand I shall not be moved. Therefore my heart is glad, and my glory rejoices; my flesh also will rest in hope.

PSALM 16:8–9 NKJV

You are my hope, O Lord GOD; You are my trust from my youth.

PSALM 71:5 NKJV

May the God of hope fill you with all joy and peace in believing, that you may abound in hope by the power of the Holy Spirit.

ROMANS 15:13 NKJV

Hope can see heaven through the thickest clouds.
—THOMAS BENTON BROOKS

In hope we count on the possibilities of the future and we do not remain imprisoned in the institutions of the past.
—JÜRGEN MOLTMANN

Humility

O Lord, It's Hard to Be Humble

My soul shall make its boast in the LORD; the humble shall hear of it and be glad.

—PSALM 34:2 NKJV

The Bible talks a lot about the importance of humility, but few seem to really understand what the concept means. After all, most men were brought up in a society that places value in things such as strength, assertiveness, and independence. From a young age, men are taught to stand up for themselves, appear confident, and never show weakness. Men learn that the person who speaks the loudest often gets what he wants the quickest. No wonder so many men believe that they should look out for themselves first before worrying about others.

The interesting thing about these values is that they run counter to the principles of humility that Jesus demonstrated to us in the Bible. As the Son of God, Jesus could have demanded that His disciples treat Him as royalty and attend to His every whim. Instead, He often humbled Himself and assumed the role of a servant to them. In one situation, He even took over the task of washing the disciples' feet, which was a job that typically fell to the lowest ranking person in the room. When the disciples protested, Jesus simply said that no servant is greater than his master and that they should follow His example.

True humility, as demonstrated by Christ, means never worrying about keeping up appearances, for no task is too low or undignified if it is done out of love for others. When you practice humility, you submit to the will of others and put their needs before your own. You put aside your desires to always be the best and instead concentrate on helping others succeed. In effect, humility means giving up those things to which you are entitled and offering them freely to someone else.

In a society where the concept of "fairness" and "self-interest" prevail, this will seem a very odd thing to do. But God wants you to put aside your pride and obediently follow the example of Christ. He wants you to admit when you have made a mistake and be willing to accept correction. Humbling yourself before others is never an easy thing to do, but it is key to following Christ's greatest commandment, to "love your neighbor as yourself."

Ask God to teach you humility and to give you a servant's heart like the one Jesus had for His disciples. In truth, it is only when you first humble yourself before God and admit that you are weak that He can then fill you with His strength and raise you up.

I Will

Allow God to show me true humility.

yes   *no*

Believe that if I humble myself, God will always
lift me up.

yes   *no*

Determine to exhibit humility in my life in all my
dealings with others.

yes   *no*

View each time I get knocked down a peg as a
lesson in humility.

yes   *no*

Remind myself to look to Christ as my model of
humility.

yes   *no*

Always remember to put others first.

yes   *no*

Things to Do

☐ *Make a list of ten ways you can begin to put the needs of others before your own.*

☐ *Read the foot-washing episode in John 13:1–17.*

☐ *Write down the names of three people who you feel live lives marked by humility.*

☐ *Make an effort to be a servant by doing something for a friend that you normally wouldn't do (such as washing that person's car or mowing his or her lawn).*

☐ *Mentally review a situation in the past where your pride flared up and caused you a problem. Write down your hindsight insights.*

☐ *Confess any areas of pride in your life to God and ask Him to help you replace your pride with humility.*

Things to Remember

All of you be submissive to one another, and be clothed with humility, for "God resists the proud, but gives grace to the humble."

1 PETER 5:5 NKJV

Jesus said, "Whoever humbles himself as this little child is the greatest in the kingdom of heaven."

MATTHEW 18:4 NKJV

Jesus said, "Whoever exalts himself will be humbled, and he who humbles himself will be exalted."

MATTHEW 23:12 NKJV

Humble yourselves under the mighty hand of God, that He may exalt you in due time.

1 PETER 5:6 NKJV

Before destruction the heart of a man is haughty, and before honor is humility.

PROVERBS 18:12 NKJV

By humility and the fear of the LORD are riches and honor and life.

—PROVERBS 22:4 NKJV

If you plan to build a tall house of virtues, you must first lay deep foundations of humility.

—SAINT AUGUSTINE OF HIPPO

Humility is not a grace that can be aquired in a few months: it is the work of a lifetime.

—FRANÇOIS FÉNELON

Obedience

Following Your Marching Orders

Keeping the commandments of God is what matters.

—DEUTERONOMY 7:19 NKJV

When people read the Bible, especially the Old Testament, and discover all the rules and regulations for obedience that God has placed there, they often begin to think of God as some heavenly ogre who has set us all up to fail. Some may even picture Him as a drill sergeant who barks out orders and then sits back to judge how well they do. Images such as these drive some people to wonder if they can ever do enough to please God.

While it is true that God wants you to obey what He has written in His Word, the idea that He is a hard-driving egomaniac is all wrong. God is a loving parent who wants you, His child, to obey for your own benefit. Just as human parents set up guidelines and rules to keep their children safe and out of trouble, God's rules are intended to guide and instruct you so that you can live a successful life.

All the rules that God established for the Israelites in the Bible were given to them because He loved them. The Ten Commandments were not written to stifle the Israelites or to boss them around. Rather, they were written to keep them safe and out of situations that would cause them to sin, fall ill, or become vulnerable to the enemies that surrounded them. Likewise, in the New Testament, Paul issued instructions to the early Christians to keep them from false teachings and to show them the true love of Christ.

You may not think that you can keep all of God's rules or even that you have the desire to do so. However, when you turn your life over to Christ, He will give you the desire to obey Him and follow His commandments. When you come up against a rule that seems outdated or unnecessarily legalistic, ask God to show you the bigger picture. What bigger purpose does the rule serve in your life and in the lives of others? What is the underlying principle or quality that the rule is intended to preserve?

As your relationship with God grows, you will begin to trust Him more and more. You will gain wisdom and understanding. Soon you will find it easier to obey. You will also find yourself obeying Him not simply to avoid the negative consequences of sin, but also to satisfy a genuine desire to please Him. In fact, you will soon discover that following your marching orders isn't quite so daunting.

I Will

Determine to believe that God always wants the best for me when He commands me to obey.

yes   *no*

Accept the fact that I don't always have to be the one in charge.

yes   *no*

Remind myself that God's rules are there for my benefit.

yes   *no*

View God as a loving parent.

yes   *no*

Trust that God will reward my obedience.

yes   *no*

Allow God to show me how to obey Him.

yes   *no*

Remember that disobedience causes pain—for me and for God.

yes   *no*

Things to Do

☐ *Ask God to show you ways that you are being disobedient to Him. Write down those things He whispers to your heart.*

☐ *List some of the misconceptions that you have had in the past about God and obedience.*

☐ *Verbally commit to a friend or spouse that you will strive to obey the Word of God.*

☐ *Think about some of the rules your parents made for you. Write a short sentence about why you think your parents wanted you to obey those rules.*

☐ *Read about God's blessings for obedience and curses for disobedience in Deuteronomy 28.*

Things to Remember

The world is passing away, and the lust of it; but he who does the will of God abides forever.

1 JOHN 2:17 NKJV

If you are willing and obedient, you shall eat the good of the land.

ISAIAH 1:19 NKJV

Observe and obey all these words which I command you, that it may go well with you and your children after you forever, when you do what is good and right in the sight of the LORD your God.

DEUTERONOMY 12:18 NKJV

Has the LORD as great delight in burnt offerings and sacrifices, as in obeying the voice of the LORD? Behold, to obey is better than sacrifice, and to heed than the fat of rams.

1 SAMUEL 15:22 NKJV

Peter and the other apostles answered and said: "We ought to obey God rather than men."

ACTS 5:29 NKJV

God is working in you, giving you the desire to obey him and the power to do what pleases him.

PHILIPPIANS 2:13 NLT

No man securely commands but he who has learned to obey.
—JOHN HOWE

The tiniest fragment of obedience, and heaven opens up and the profoundest truths of God are yours straight away.
—OSWALD CHAMBERS

Integrity

Living Life Right When No One's Looking

You are witnesses, and God also, how devoutly and justly and blamelessly we behaved ourselves among you who believe.

—1 THESSALONIANS 2:10 NKJV

Most people define a person of integrity as one who has a high ethical standard and who generally chooses to do things in an honest way. Yet integrity involves much more than just having an ethical code or being honest in certain situations.

Integrity means choosing to consistently do the right thing in every situation and live each day according to the ethics defined by Christ Himself. It means not shading the truth or cutting corners to get ahead because it is easier. When you live a life of integrity, you don't just do things to keep up appearances. What others see on the outside must always reflect what is truly on the inside.

Living a life according to these standards is a tough thing to do, and many people in the public eye have failed and have been forced to suffer the consequences. In May 1998, an associate editor from the *New Republic* was fired after the magazine learned that he had fabricated information in twenty-seven out of the forty-one articles he'd written for them. In June 1998, a *Boston Globe* columnist was forced to give up an industry award when it was discovered that she had made up people and quotes used in her column. In December 2001, the new head coach of a large university resigned from his position after five days when numerous inaccuracies in his résumé began to surface.

Given these examples, it is obvious that one reason to live a life of integrity is to avoid the humiliation that results when dishonesty surfaces. However, there are many more reasons to live an honest and aboveboard life. Integrity brings with it a sense of inner peace and confidence. It will enhance your relationship with God and open you to the trust of those around us. Guard your integrity; think before you act.

When you fail—and you will fail at times—remember that the test of integrity is not perfection but a willingness to admit your mistakes. When you find yourself in a situation where your integrity has been compromised, go straight to God and ask Him to forgive you. Then go and make it right with those you have been dishonest with. Above all, continually ask God to show you how to live a better and more honest life. It's the most important thing a man can do.

I Will

Allow God to reveal areas of my life where I lack
integrity.   *yes*   *no*
                                                                _____   _____

Determine to live in integrity in my relationships
with others.   *yes*   *no*
                                                                _____   _____

Accept that I will make mistakes, but not be afraid
to admit those mistakes.   *yes*   *no*
                                                                _____   _____

Believe that practicing true integrity is the best
way to live.   *yes*   *no*
                                                                _____   _____

Realize that others look to me as a role model and
take that responsibility seriously.   *yes*   *no*
                                                                _____   _____

Trust that God will help me as I strive to live a life
of integrity.   *yes*   *no*
                                                                _____   _____

Things to Do

☐ *Identify any gray areas that you might have in your life and ask God
to help you discern what is right from wrong in these areas. Be sure to
write them down.*

☐ *Think of two to three times that you know you've cut corners and
behaved unethically. Meditate on how you could have handled those
situations differently and how you feel they would have come out.*

☐ *Write out an action plan for how you will live with integrity in the
future.*

☐ *Memorize Proverbs 11:3—"The integrity of the upright will guide them,
but the perversity of the unfaithful will destroy them."*

☐ *Write out a prayer asking God to help you to be honest in everything
you do.*

Things to Remember

He who walks with integrity walks securely, but he who perverts his ways will become known.

PROVERBS 10:9 NKJV

The righteous man walks in his integrity; his children are blessed after him.

PROVERBS 20:7 NKJV

As for me, You uphold me in my integrity, and set me before Your face forever.

PSALM 41:12 NKJV

The integrity of good people creates a safe place for living.

PROVERBS 14:3 THE MESSAGE

Exhort the young men to be sober-minded, in all things showing yourself to be a pattern of good works; in doctrine showing integrity, reverence, incorruptibility, sound speech that cannot be condemned, that one who is an opponent may be ashamed, having nothing evil to say of you.

TITUS 2:6–8 NKJV

There is no such thing as a minor lapse of integrity.

—TOM PETERS

Integrity can be neither lost nor concealed nor faked nor quenched nor artificially come by nor outlived, nor, I believe, in the long run denied.

—EUDORA WELTY

Salvation

The Only Way

Jesus answered and said to him, "Most assuredly, I say to you, unless one is born again, he cannot see the kingdom of God."

—JOHN 3:3 NKJV

Most people believe that heaven is a place of eternal happiness where good people go after they die. The question is, what makes a good person? Some people believe that they can secure their place in heaven by doing a lot of good deeds. Others think the way to get in is to live a good life, as perceived by the values of society. Some think the way is through meditation and inner enlightenment. Still others think that one is good only if he or she adheres to a strict set of rules and guidelines.

Consider the meanness and the hurts that you see inflicted by some people. Then consider the kindness and compassion that you see practiced by caring people toward everyone with whom they come in contact. This reads like what is popularly called a *no-brainer*—it sure doesn't require much thought to determine which of the two types of people is more worthy of heaven. But you know the answer to that already, right? Neither type is worthy.

The problem is that you can never be good enough to earn your way into heaven. If you think you will go to heaven just because you're a good person—forget about it! Heaven is more than just a place for good people to go when they die; it is in fact the dwelling place of God. To enter into heaven means to enter into the presence of God, which is something that no one who has ever committed even one sin during his or her lifetime can do. The dilemma here is that according to the Bible, *everyone* has sinned and fallen short of the glory of God. No one qualifies.

God cannot endure sin. He doesn't sweep it under the rug or pretend it doesn't exist. Because of His incredible love, however, He has provided a way for you to enter into His presence and receive eternal life. The cost was high, for the only way to cleanse you of your sin was to send His Son Jesus into the world to bear the sins of all humankind. As an ultimate gesture of love, He allowed His Son to be crucified as a sacrifice for your sins, so that through Him you could receive salvation and enter into His presence.

Take advantage of God's goodness by receiving the priceless free gift He offers you. To receive it, all you have to do is believe that Jesus died for your sins, and then confess those sins to God. God will cleanse you and make you holy in His sight. He will not only give you eternal life, but He will also give you new values and a new reason for living. He will make you a part of His family and give you the strength to follow Him.

I Will

Believe that through Christ I can be saved.   _yes_   _no_

Realize that I can never earn salvation.   _yes_   _no_

Remember that Christ paid the ultimate price as a
cost for my sin.   _yes_   _no_

Exhibit the joy of God's salvation in my life.   _yes_   _no_

Accept that I am imperfect and that I have sinned,
but that God can forgive me.   _yes_   _no_

Allow God to reveal areas of sin in my life.   _yes_   _no_

Trust in God's Word when it says that if I believe in
Christ and follow Him, I will one day be with Him in
heaven.   _yes_   _no_

Things to Do

☐ *Write out a prayer asking God to give you His values for your life and
the strength to follow Him.*

☐ *Talk to a friend and get his or her views on what heaven is and how to
get there.*

☐ *Pray for a friend or family member who needs God's gift of salvation.*

☐ *Memorize 1 Thessalonians 5:9—"God did not appoint us to wrath, but
to obtain salvation through our Lord Jesus Christ."*

☐ *List some of the ways you have tried to show God and others that you
are a "good" person.*

☐ *Read Jesus' prayer for Himself, His disciples, and all believers just prior
to His death on the cross in John 17.*

Things to Remember

Jesus said, "I am the way, the truth, and the life. No one comes to the Father except through Me."

JOHN 14:6 NKJV

All have sinned; all fall short of God's glorious standard. Yet now God in his gracious kindness declares us not guilty. He has done this through Christ Jesus, who has freed us.

ROMANS 3:23–24 NLT

God our Savior showed us his kindness and love. He saved us, not because of the good things we did, but because of his mercy. He washed away our sins and gave us a new life through the Holy Spirit.

TITUS 3:4–5 NLT

He made Him who knew no sin to be sin for us, that we might become the righteousness of God in Him.

2 CORINTHIANS 5:21 NKJV

By grace you have been saved through faith, and that not of yourselves; it is the gift of God, not of works, lest anyone should boast.

EPHESIANS 2:8–9 NKJV

Man needs, above all else, salvation. He needs to turn round and see that God is standing there with a rope ready to throw to him if only he will catch it and attach it to himself.

—NORMAN GOODACRE

There is no more urgent and critical question in life than that of your personal relationship with God and your eternal salvation.

—BILLY GRAHAM

Self-Esteem

The Great Creator

The Mighty One, God the Lord, has spoken and called the earth from the rising of the sun to its going down.

—PSALM 50:1–2 NKJV

If you ever looked up into the branches of a sturdy oak, stood in the wet sand as the vast blue sea laps at your feet, gazed up at the sky on a clear, star-filled night, taken in the rich fragrance of a beautiful flower, or stood spellbound as the sun passed across the peak of a snow-capped mountain, then you have experienced the wonder and awe of God's Creation. Nature is His handiwork, the Bible says.

In the very beginning, before creation, there was nothingness. Genesis aptly describes this: "Darkness was on the face of the deep" (1:2 NKJV). Then God began His awesome work. By merely speaking the words, He created light and flooded the earth with sunlight. He divided light from darkness and gave the world day and night.

God is the creator and ruler of all the marvels in the world. The Bible says that He created the heavens and the earth, the waters and the land, the animals and the plants—and He saw that it was good. He created man as well, in His own image. You are the crowning achievement of God's creative genius. Believe that.

Each time you look out and marvel at the wonders around you, take time to appreciate more fully what you mean to God. Formed by His own hand in His own image, you are linked to Him forever. He has given you a free will, believing that you will choose to love Him. And when people did not love God and turned their backs on their creator, God turned the tables in heaven and on earth to open the door once more, to see that the way to relationship with Him was not blocked.

It's easy in a world that has become increasingly impersonal and uncaring for men to doubt that they have value, especially to God. If you have come to feel that way, look up—at the trees, at the stars, at the wonders of God all around you. Then consider the fact that God values you more than anything else He has created. He has invested more of Himself in you than in the most beautiful sunset or that exquisite snow-white owl hooting majestically in the distance.

You are so valuable to Him, in fact, that He has chosen to call you His child. Look around you today, and then consider who you are and what you mean to God. Receive His love, let it wash over you, let it speak to you and lift you up. Then as you experience His love, open your heart to love Him in return. He has been waiting a long time.

I Will

Appreciate the wonder of God's creation in nature. _____ yes _____ no

Believe that God is the author and creator of all things. _____ yes _____ no

Realize that God has created beautiful things in this world to demonstrate His love and care for me. _____ yes _____ no

Accept myself as a part of God's wonderful creation. _____ yes _____ no

Allow God to open my eyes and help me see that I am the masterpiece of His creation. _____ yes _____ no

Allow myself to respond to the love of God. _____ yes _____ no

Determine to return God's will as a function of my free will. _____ yes _____ no

Things to Do

☐ Plan a short walk in the park or a hike in the woods.

☐ Write a short paragraph about the beauty you see in nature.

☐ Write out a prayer asking God to help you appreciate the beauty of His creation.

☐ Put a note on your refrigerator or bathroom mirror that says "I am created in the image of God!"

☐ Write a short song or poem extolling God's creative genius.

☐ Memorize 1 John 3:1—"Behold what manner of love the Father has bestowed on us, that we should be called children of God."

Things to Remember

The heavens declare the glory of God; and the firmament shows His handiwork.

PSALM 19:1 NKJV

God created man in His own image; in the image of God He created him; male and female He created them.

GENESIS 1:27 NKJV

Jesus said, "Are not two sparrows sold for a copper coin? And not one of them falls to the ground apart from your Father's will. But the very hairs of your head are all numbered. Do not fear therefore; you are of more value than many sparrows."

MATTHEW 10:29–31 NKJV

You did not receive the spirit of bondage again to fear, but you received the Spirit of adoption by whom we cry out, "Abba, Father." The Spirit Himself bears witness with our spirit that we are children of God, and if children, then heirs—heirs of God and joint heirs with Christ.

ROMANS 8:15–17 NKJV

The earth is the LORD's, and all its fullness, the world and those who dwell therein.

PSALM 24:1 NKJV

It is difficult to make a man miserable while he feels worthy of himself and claims kindred to the great God who made him.

—ABRAHAM LINCOLN

People who do not experience self-love have little or no capacity to love others.

—NATHANIEL BRANDEN

Forgiving Others

The First Step

Put up with each other, and forgive anyone who does you wrong, just as Christ has forgiven you.

—Colossians 3:13 CEV

God is always willing and able to forgive no matter what you have done or how many times you have done it. Out of His incredible grace and mercy, God offers His gift of forgiveness to anyone who asks. The only thing that He requires in return is that you offer this same gift to others.

Of course, no one has the grace and patience of God, and forgiving others can be a real problem at times. This is especially true when the same person keeps doing things to hurt you over and over again. In the Bible, Peter asked Jesus, "How many times shall I forgive my brother when he sins against me? Up to seven times?" The rabbis of Christ's time taught that you had to forgive someone up to three times before getting even with them. However, Jesus' answer was "seventy times seven." In other words, "Quit counting, Peter."

Why does God put this condition on forgiveness? One

reason is certainly so that the concept of forgiveness can be understood and that God's gift of forgiveness will not be taken lightly. But perhaps another reason is that God knows the emotional and physical damage that holding a grudge can cause.

In a study conducted by the University of Michigan in 2001, researchers found that people who forgive others tend to be more satisfied with their lives and less likely to report symptoms of psychological distress such as restlessness, nervousness, or sadness. A University of Wisconsin study found that people who forgive less often tend to have more diseases and report more medical symptoms. In an article published by the *Seattle Times*, Robert Enright, professor of education psychology at the university, stated, "We've been surprised at how strong forgiveness can be as a healing agent for people." Similar studies also show that the ability to forgive can greatly enhance personal relationships.

From this evidence, you can see that forgiving others has many benefits. That doesn't make it any easier to do, however. How do you forgive and forget? Remind yourself that you, too, need forgiveness, and that God has given it unsparingly. Then choose not to dwell on the hurt and pain that the other person has caused you. Give it up to God and let Him heal you and show you the power of forgiveness. In this way, you can truly follow the words of the apostle Paul in the book of Colossians and "forgive as the Lord forgave you."

I Will

Believe that God wants me to forgive others as He
has forgiven me.   _yes_   _no_

Realize the damage that holding a grudge can cause.   _yes_   _no_

View situations where others sin against me as a
chance to demonstrate Christ's forgiveness.   _yes_   _no_

Accept God's forgiveness in my life and share it with
others.   _yes_   _no_

Allow God to show me ways to forgive others.   _yes_   _no_

Trust in the promise that if I forgive others, God will
forgive me.   _yes_   _no_

Always remember the healing power of forgiveness.   _yes_   _no_

Things to Do

☐ *Write out a prayer asking God to help you to forgive others.*

☐ *Think of an instance when somebody wronged you. Tell God how it
made you feel, and then forgive them.*

☐ *Memorize Colossians 3:13: "Put up with each other, and forgive anyone
who does you wrong, just as Christ has forgiven you" (CEV).*

☐ *Ask God to reveal any grudges that you may be holding against another
person.*

☐ *Read Jesus' Parable of the Unmerciful Servant in Matthew 18:21–35.*

☐ *Set a time to reflect on each day's events and determine if you need to
forgive anyone who has wronged you.*

Things to Remember

Jesus said, "Take heed to yourselves. If your brother sins against you, rebuke him; and if he repents, forgive him. And if he sins against you seven times in a day, and seven times in a day returns to you, saying, 'I repent,' you shall forgive him."

LUKE 17:3–4 NKJV

Jesus prayed, "Our Father in heaven, hallowed be Your name. . . . Forgive us our debts, as we forgive our debtors."

MATTHEW 6:9, 12 NKJV

Jesus said, "Judge not, and you shall not be judged. Condemn not, and you shall not be condemned. Forgive, and you will be forgiven."

LUKE 6:37 NKJV

Confess your trespasses to one another, and pray for one another, that you may be healed. The effective, fervent prayer of a righteous man avails much.

JAMES 5:16 NKJV

Be kind to one another, tenderhearted, forgiving one another, even as God in Christ forgave you.

EPHESIANS 4:32 NKJV

> The only true forgiveness is that which is offered and extended even before the offender has apologized and sought it.
> —SØREN KIERKEGAARD

> When you forgive, you in no way change the past— but you sure do change the future.
> —BERNARD MELTZER

Perseverance

Life Is a Marathon, Not a Sprint

Let us hold fast the confession of our hope without wavering, for He who promised is faithful.

—HEBREWS 10:23 NKJV

The apostle Paul compared a person living a godly life to that of an athlete running a race. Like the athlete who must train hard to have physical stamina to finish the race that he is running, the man who wishes to live a life pleasing to God must train hard to have spiritual stamina. He must have perseverance.

Perseverance means trusting God and consistently following His ways because you know that He will stand beside you and help get you through the toughest times in life. The remarkable thing about perseverance is that it makes you focus on the prize rather than on the obstacles that stand in your way. When you focus on the reward and think about all the incredible things God has promised you when this life is over, you can't help but be optimistic about the future.

It's easy when you first turn your life over to God to dive headlong into the Bible and spend hours in prayer in order to grow in the Lord as quickly as possible. That's a good thing, but you must remember that as time passes, the excitement will fade somewhat and the newness of your experience will wear off. It takes time and patience and commitment to develop godly character. But, as so many have discovered before you, including the apostle Paul, it will be worth it when you hear God say, "Well done." So don't let yourself get winded after the first sprint and give up. Stay in the race until you have won the prize.

It is important to remember that life is a marathon, not a sprint, and that there are things you can do to develop perseverance. Start off small by developing daily habits like reading a few chapters from the Bible or spending a few minutes in prayer. Don't try to do too much at once or give up at the first sign of failure. Try to fellowship with other people who have a relationship with God when you can, for through them you will gain support and encouragement. When you finally have time to look back at the course at the end, you will be amazed at how far you have come and be glad you stayed the course.

Everyone who crosses the finish line of that race gets the prize. The important thing is that you get there.

I Will

Accept the fact that living a life for God requires
perseverance.

yes   *no*

Allow God to strengthen me when I am weary and
want to give up.

yes   *no*

View life as a marathon, not as a sprint.

yes   *no*

Believe that God will help me to persevere.

yes   *no*

Exhibit patience and commitment in my life.

yes   *no*

Remember that God's schedule for my spiritual
growth is often different from my own.

yes   *no*

Trust that God will bring others into my life to give
me support and encouragement.

yes   *no*

Things to Do

☐ *Share a personal struggle with a friend or spouse and ask them to help you persevere.*

☐ *Make a personal commitment to develop habits that will help you persevere in your relationship with God (such as attending church regularly or spending time each day reading the Bible).*

☐ *Write out a prayer asking God to help you persevere in living a life that is pleasing to Him.*

☐ *Look for and encourage someone who is struggling to endure some hardship or overcome a bad habit.*

☐ *Watch the 1993 movie Rudy about perseverance and determination in the face of overwhelming obstacles.*

Things to Remember

My beloved brethren, be steadfast, immovable, always abounding in the work of the Lord, knowing that your labor is not in vain in the Lord.

1 CORINTHIANS 15:58 NKJV

In the Parable of the Talents, Jesus said, "His lord said to him, 'Well done, good and faithful servant; you were faithful over a few things, I will make you ruler over many things. Enter into the joy of your lord.'"

MATTHEW 25:21 NKJV

We desire that each one of you show the same diligence to the full assurance of hope until the end, that you do not become sluggish, but imitate those who through faith and patience inherit the promises.

HEBREWS 6:11–12 NKJV

Let us not grow weary while doing good, for in due season we shall reap if we do not lose heart.

GALATIANS 6:9 NKJV

We have become partakers of Christ if we hold the beginning of our confidence steadfast to the end.

HEBREWS 3:14 NKJV

Perseverance is the sister of patience, the daughter of constancy, the friend of peace, the cementer of friendships, the bond of harmony and bulwark of holiness.

—BERNARD OF CLAIRVAUX

Perseverance is not a long race; it is many short races one after another.

—DR. V. RAYMOND EDMAN

An Overflowing Heart

Oh, give thanks to the God of gods! For His mercy endures forever.

—Psalm 136:1 NKJV

A man's world can easily become bogged down with the minutia of everyday living—managing multiple responsibilities, seeing to the needs of others, and so much more. It's a balancing act. But no matter how busy you get—how many promotions you go after, deals you need to close, credit cards you need to pay off, preteen soccer games you need to attend, leaky faucets you need to fix—don't forget to thank God from your heart for all the blessings He has brought into your life.

Most people learned as children to say "please" and "thank you." It might have been that way with you, too, your parents hammering it home every chance they got. Now as a man, you may find yourself still saying thank you as a polite response when a cashier hands you your change or a server brings you your meal. It has probably become such a habit that you hardly think about it. It's a good thing to continue the polite practice of saying thank you. But it's even better when that thankfulness comes from your heart.

So how do you nurture a truly thankful heart? As you may have learned from your parents, practice makes perfect. Choose to consciously look around you every day and acknowledge the good things God has placed in your life. Do you have a family? Be thankful. Do you have a job, a means of earning a living? Be thankful. Do you have food on the table? A warm coat in the winter? Be thankful. Can you see? Hear? Walk? Breathe? Are you alive? Be thankful. Can you feel the breeze and enjoy the beauty of a flower? Be thankful. Have you accepted God's gift of salvation? Be thankful. Come on! Once you get started, you'll find an endless list of things to be thankful for.

In order to nurture a truly thankful heart, it's also important to thank God in the tough times as well as the good times. Maybe you have recently lost a loved one. Choose to be thankful for his or her life and the time you were able to spend together. Perhaps you've experienced a personal illness. Choose to thank God for allowing you to learn through that experience, so you can help others who are suffering with pain and sickness. Maybe the brakes have gone out on the car— again. Choose to thank God that you have a car. Were you passed over for a promotion? Choose to thank God that His timing is perfect and that He will not open a door until He knows you are ready to go through it.

Being thankful isn't just a nice thing to do. It is a biblical principle. The apostle Paul urged his fellow believers to give thanks in all circumstances, for that was God's will for them

(1 Thessalonians 5:18). He didn't encourage them to make a list of their troubles. He did not say to be thankful only as a polite gesture to others. He did not say to thank God only for the good things in life. Paul's message was to look around them and give thanks in the midst of every situation that came their way.

Perhaps God puts so much stock in being thankful because of the many benefits a thankful heart can bring to your life. It can strengthen your relationships. It can ward off depression and sadness. It can rescue you from pride and arrogance. And it can help you realize that God, in His infinite wisdom and grace, has given you more than you deserve or could ever hope to achieve on your own. Most of all, it will keep you from overlooking the great gift of salvation that God has provided and your need for it. A thankful attitude puts you in your place, and lifts God to His place, as your benevolent heavenly Father.

So make it your choice to count your blessings every day—remembering to include those blessings disguised as challenges. And as you go about your counting, remember to say thank you to your Creator. Then say it again and again and again—in every circumstance. That is God's will for you.

As members of one body you are all called to live in peace. And always be thankful.

—Colossians 3:15 NLT

I Will

Allow my thankful attitude to help strengthen my relationship with God.

yes   _no_

Reflect on the blessings and challenges in my life and be thankful.

yes   _no_

Strive to accept the thanks of others in a humble manner.

yes   _no_

Exhibit a thankful attitude to others.

yes   _no_

Impress upon others the importance of thanking God as a regular practice.

yes   _no_

Maintain a thankful attitude with others, acknowledging them verbally.

yes   _no_

Things to Do

☐ _Make a list of five things that you consider to be blessings in your life._

☐ _Make another list of five things that you consider to be challenges or difficulties in your life._

☐ _Write out a prayer thanking God for all ten items listed._

☐ _Call a friend or loved one and thank him or her for a kind act that was directed toward you._

☐ _Memorize 1 Thessalonians 5:18—"In everything give thanks; for this is the will of God in Christ Jesus for you."_

☐ _Write a thank-you note to the next person who does an unexpected favor for you._

Things to Remember

May you be filled with joy, always thanking the Father, who has enabled you to share the inheritance that belongs to God's holy people, who live in the light.

COLOSSIANS 1:11–12 NLT

Let us come before His presence with thanksgiving; let us shout joyfully to Him with psalms. For the LORD is the great God, and the great King above all gods.

PSALM 95:2–3 NKJV

Let us continually offer the sacrifice of praise to God, that is, the fruit of our lips, giving thanks to His name.
—Hebrews 13:15 NKJV

I will praise the name of God with a song, and will magnify Him with thanksgiving. This also shall please the LORD.

PSALM 69:30–31 NKJV

Enter into His gates with thanksgiving, and into His courts with praise. Be thankful to Him, and bless His name.

PSALM 100:4 NKJV

Oh, give thanks to the LORD, for He is good! For His mercy endures forever.

PSALM 107:1 NKJV

I exhort first of all that supplications, prayers, intercessions, and giving of thanks be made for all men, for kings and all who are in authority, that we may lead a quiet and peaceable life in all godliness and reverence.

1 TIMOTHY 2:1–2 NKJV

Sing praise to the LORD, you saints of His, and give thanks at the remembrance of His holy name.

PSALM 30:4 NKJV

I will give You thanks in the great assembly; I will praise You among many people.

PSALM 35:18 NKJV

The LORD said to Moses, "When you offer a sacrifice of thanksgiving to the LORD, offer it of your own free will."

LEVITICUS 22:29 NKJV

LORD, accept my grateful thanks and teach me your laws.

PSALM 119:108 NLT

Since evrything God created is good, we should not reject any of it. We may receive it gladly, with thankful hearts.

1 TIMOTHY 4:4 NLT

One act of thanksgiving when things go wrong with us is worth a thousand thanks when things are agreeable in words or works.

—J. B. LIGHTFOOT

The Christian is suspended between blessings received and blessings hoped for, so he should always give thanks.

—MARVIN RICHARDSON VINCENT

Want to Be Set Free?

I have chosen the way of truth; Your judgments I have laid before me.

—Psalm 119:30 NKJV

What does it mean to say "The truth shall set you free"? There are many freedoms—the freedom to live anywhere, the freedom to earn and spend money, the freedom to marry and have a family or remain single, the freedom to choose a career. But the truth about freedom is that it comes with a price tag, and that price is responsibility.

Some men have tried to practice freedom without responsibility and found themselves trapped in a web of sexual addiction, gambling, or a number of other vices. Recognizing the truth and taking responsibility for their actions is the first step toward true freedom for these men. The second step is to let go of their freedom and give themselves to God.

There is a tribe in South America whose members have a unique way of catching monkeys. A large gourd with a long narrow neck is secured in an area frequented by monkeys. Fruit is placed in the gourd and then left there.

A monkey catches a whiff of the tempting fruit and wanders in closer to the gourd. He looks into the gourd and sees something he wants—fruit. Sticking his arm through the narrow opening, the monkey will reach to the bottom of the gourd, grab the fruit and start to remove his arm. But he is stuck—trapped in the gourd because his once opened hand is now a fist that will not fit through the narrow opening.

Unfortunately for most monkeys trapped in this situation, they do not think to let go of the fruit. Instead, they struggle and pull and try to get their fist out because they refuse to let go of what they desire to have. Their appetite takes over and they continue to clench their fist. The end result for the monkey is death.

How many men are like the monkeys in South America? What are you holding on to that prevents your freedom? Are there any desires, appetites, or addictions that need to be dealt with? Is there something in your life that is keeping you trapped? God provides a solution—His love and forgiveness. Recognize the truth of your problem, then let go of it and give it to God. No one is making you keep your fist clenched tightly. It's your choice, and the truth shall set you free!

I Will

Recognize that freedom without responsibility is
bondage.

yes   no

Allow God to teach me about true freedom.

yes   no

Endeavor to cling to God instead of clinging to what
tempts me away from Him.

yes   no

Submit my freedom to God.

yes   no

Nurture in myself a repentant heart.

yes   no

Encourage those who are learning hard lessons
about freedom.

yes   no

Remember that the truth is what brings freedom.

yes   no

Things to Do

☐ Make a list of those things that you allow yourself to be trapped by.

☐ Burn the list and thank God for His deliverance from those areas you
identified.

☐ The next time you are tempted to sin, hold your hands open—no
clenched fists—as a reminder to yourself to follow God's leading.

☐ If your struggle is a physical one such as overeating, alcoholism, sexual
addiction, or gambling, seek an outside counseling program for help.

☐ Find a counselor, friend, or pastor who can guide you on your course to
freedom.

☐ Memorize John 8:32—"You shall know the truth, and the truth shall
make you free."

Things to Remember

Jesus said, "You shall know the truth, and the truth shall make you free."

JOHN 8:32 NKJV

Sin shall not have dominion over you, for you are not under law but under grace. What then? Shall we sin because we are not under law but under grace? Certainly not!

ROMANS 6:14–15 NKJV

Stand fast therefore in the liberty by which Christ has made us free, and do not be entangled again with a yoke of bondage.

GALATIANS 5:1 NKJV

I beseech you therefore, brethren, by the mercies of God, that you present your bodies a living sacrifice, holy, acceptable to God, which is your reasonable service.

ROMANS 12:1 NKJV

I can do anything I want to if Christ has not said no, but some of these things aren't good for me. Even if I am allowed to do them, I'll refuse to if I think they might get such a grip on me that I can't easily stop when I want to.

1 CORINTHIANS 6:12 TLB

Set me free from evil passions, and heal my heart of all inordinate affections; that being inwardly cured and thoroughly cleansed, I may be made fit to love, courageous to suffer, stead to persevere.

THOMAS À KEMPIS

The spirit of truth and the spirit of freedom—they are the pillars of society.

—HENRIK IBSEN

Adventure

Leaving Your Comfort Zone Behind

Have I not commanded you? Be strong and of good courage; do not be afraid, nor be dismayed, for the LORD your God is with you wherever you go.

—JOSHUA 1:9 NKJV

Life is an adventure! Sometimes the adventure makes the man, and sometimes the man makes the adventure. But either way, there comes a time in each man's life when he must step out of the familiar and try something new—leaving his comfort zone behind.

Have you ever stopped to think that many of Jesus' disciples were simple, hardworking men who fished for a living? Then one day Jesus came walking along the shore of the Sea of Galilee and beckoned them to follow Him. When they laid down their nets and left their boats behind, their lives changed drastically. Soon they were traveling from one end of the land to the other. They witnessed miracles and saw lives changed forever in an instant. They witnessed the transfiguration of Jesus, as well as His crucifixion and resurrection. It couldn't have been easy for them to walk away from the only lives they had ever known. But the amazing things they experienced as they followed Jesus through the countryside made it all worthwhile.

And what about Noah? When he was 600 years old, God asked him to build an ark, fill it with animals, and ride out a global flood. But Noah wasn't deterred by his age or the fact that no one but his immediate family believed in his endeavor. He hammered away while the sun shone and his neighbors jeered. Now imagine how he must have felt when that first raindrop plopped down on his tough, sun-baked skin.

Moses was a reluctant leader with a stutter. Egypt had been a comfortable place for a long time, but things changed. As conditions became more and more unbearable, Moses answered God's call to lead His people away from Egypt to an unknown land where they would be safe and blessed. He led them right through the center of the Red Sea, with towering walls of water on either side.

David threw aside the king's armor and faced a giant with only his sling and five smooth stones. That meant leaving his comfortable job looking after the sheep and heading for the battlefield. But David was willing, and one day the shepherd boy became the king.

Your life changes may not be quite so dramatic, but who's to say—they could be! There may come a time when God taps you on the shoulder and asks you to leave your comfort zone behind. You might get the opportunity to try something new and to learn and grow as you chase after God's will. God probably won't ask you to build an ark, but He might ask you to help build an important company and carry the responsibility for meeting the needs of your customers and employees. Or He might ask you to go to a foreign land in pursuit of those who have not yet heard the good news that Jesus died for their sins.

Maybe you are a reluctant leader like Moses, unsure of your ability, but you too can be used of God to bring others through tough times. You may not be adept with a sling, but using your God-given talents and skills can strengthen you to conquer the biggest of problems.

Your path from the comfort zone may come as a direct assignment from God, as it did for the Bible characters mentioned above, or He may allow you to choose your own great adventure. All it takes is a willingness to leave your comfortable routines behind and take a chance.

Where do you begin? Simply by trying something new. Take up a new sport, learn a new language, tackle a new hobby. You could learn to play an instrument or join the choir. You could take a trip to someplace where you have never been. Ask God to reveal to you gifts and talents you don't even know you have. Open your heart to change, to new possibilities. Don't sit around watching other people as they reap the benefits of an adventurous life—live your own.

God has created an amazing world filled with spectacular vistas and thrilling experiences. Trouble is, they are difficult to spot from the comfort of your easy chair. So turn off the television, open your eyes, listen to God, and get moving— start discovering the adventure that is right in front of you.

I Will

Exhibit an adventurous attitude in my life.   *yes*   *no*

Look for experiences that cause me to grow
and learn.   *yes*   *no*

Consider the adventurous option when faced
with two possible choices.   *yes*   *no*

Allow God to take me into areas outside my
comfort zone.   *yes*   *no*

Encourage others who are struggling to leave
their comfort zones.   *yes*   *no*

Enjoy the gift of life.   *yes*   *no*

Things to Do

☐ *Write out a prayer asking God to show you the adventures in life.*

☐ *Make a list of things to try that are outside of your comfort zone.*

☐ *Pick one item off of that list that you can begin today.*

☐ *Take a different route home from work.*

☐ *Volunteer to help out one time with an organization such as Meals on Wheels or the Salvation Army.*

☐ *Travel someplace that you have never been to before and take a friend to share the experience with you.*

☐ *Turn off the television for an entire weekend.*

Things to Remember

This Book of the Law shall not depart from your mouth, but you shall meditate in it day and night, that you may observe to do according to all that is written in it. For then you will make your way prosperous, and then you will have good success.

JOSHUA 1:8 NKJV

By faith Abraham obeyed when he was called to go out to the place which he would receive as an inheritance. And he went out, not knowing where he was going.

HEBREWS 11:8 NKJV

Jesus said to her, "Daughter, you took a risk of faith, and now you're healed and whole. Live well, live blessed! Be healed of your plague."
—Mark 5:34 THE MESSAGE

Jesus said, "Go therefore and make disciples of all the nations, baptizing them in the name of the Father and of the Son and of the Holy Spirit, teaching them to observe all things that I have commanded you; and lo, I am with you always, even to the end of the age."

MATTHEW 28:19–20 NKJV

He said to them, "Follow Me, and I will make you fishers of men." They immediately left their nets and followed Him.

MATTHEW 4:19–20 NKJV

I, the LORD your God, will hold your right hand, saying to you, "Fear not, I will help you."

ISAIAH 41:13 NKJV

Peter went over the side of the boat and walked on the water toward Jesus. But when he looked around at the high waves, he was terrified and began to sink. "Save me, Lord!" he shouted. Instantly Jesus reached out his hand and rescued him.

MATTHEW 14:29–31 TLB

The LORD said, "Fear not, for I have redeemed you; I have called you by your name; you are Mine."

ISAIAH 43:1 NKJV

When you go through deep waters and great trouble, I will be with you. When you go through rivers of difficulty, you will not drown! When you walk through the fire of oppression, you will not be burned up—the flames will not consume you. For I am the Lord your God, your Savior.

ISAIAH 43:2–3 TLB

It is only in adventure that some people succeed in knowing themselves—in finding themselves.

—ANDRÉ GIDE

An adventure is only an inconvenience rightly considered. An inconvenience is only an adventure wrongly considered.

—G. K. CHESTERTON

Learning to Walk a Tightrope

Take up the whole armor of God, that you may be able to withstand in the evil day, and having done all, to stand.

EPHESIANS 6:13 NKJV

Balance is a word that means many things to many people. A tightrope walker might imagine the feel of a taut cable beneath his feet. A manager might remember balancing his annual budget. A judge might envision the fair scales of justice. A politician might reflect on the checks and balances of the branches of government.

What does it mean for you personally? Balancing your car tires? Balancing your checkbook? What about balancing your life? What constitutes a balanced life anyway?

Imbalance may be easier to spot in someone else's life than in your own. But no matter how the exercise turns out, self-diagnosis will at least let you see how you're doing. Following are just a few of the questions you should ask yourself:

How strong is my relationship with God, with my spouse, with my children?

How well is my career progressing?

How well do I get along with my coworkers?

Are my finances in order?

How well do I make and keep friends?

Is godly character evident in my life?

Am I caring for the needs of my body and mind?

Do I maintain a sense of inner joy and well-being, despite my outward circumstances?

Once you've made a valid assessment of your balance sheet, resist the urge to go for quick fixes like promising yourself you will spend more time with your family and less time at work, attend church more regularly, find time for yourself, or head back to the gym. These are good things of course. But good intentions won't go far unless you're willing to make deeper changes—heart changes.

Heart changes are the kind that come from living life, all of life, with God at your side. Surrendering your will to God's will is the most important piece in the foundation of a balanced life. God has a plan and purpose for every life. Ask Him to reveal what that purpose is for you. God will provide all you need to help you succeed as long as you have the courage to walk in the steps He's ordained for you.

What does a balanced life look like? No two lives are alike. But one thing is certain: A balanced life is full of motion, action, and response to change. As you surrender your will and live your life with God by your side, God will reveal His plan for you. And it's a good bet that His plan will require some action on your part.

Unless you prefer spinning your wheels on a stationary bike or riding one with training wheels, it's almost impossible to balance on a bicycle that's standing still. But when you start pedaling and rolling forward, balance becomes easier. Of course you will still need to make adjustments and respond to changes in the road, but balance will be achieved through action.

A tightrope walker is never perfectly still. If you watch him closely, he is constantly adjusting his body, a slight arm movement here, a tip of the pole there, a leg kicking out and then back in. He uses all the muscles in his body. He is always moving, yet he is balanced. He also uses specific tools to help him stay balanced. He wears soft-soled shoes so he can feel the rope or cable with his feet. He carries a long pole or some similar apparatus to help him maintain his center of gravity. If the line sways or the wind blows, the tightrope walker uses his tools, along with his God-given abilities, to maintain balance and accomplish the task of walking the rope.

Look at your life. Are your priorities in order? Are you living your life in accordance with God's will? What areas of your life are out of balance? Once you have determined that—act. Make a list of the steps you can take to make the necessary correction. Be open to let God use you in ways you never dreamed. Be confident and know that God will bring you into balance as you surrender your life to Him. It may not happen overnight, but you can learn to walk the tightrope of life with confidence.

I Will

Live according to God's will in all areas of my life.   _yes_   _no_

Stay grounded in my personal relationship
with Jesus.   _yes_   _no_

Consider another person's welfare before my
own desires.   _yes_   _no_

Relate to those around me by exhibiting a
selfless love.   _yes_   _no_

Identify those areas of my life that do not conform
to godly character.   _yes_   _no_

Allow God to use me to serve the needs of others.   _yes_   _no_

Things to Do

☐ Ask God to help you balance the priorities in your life.

☐ Find someone trustworthy who will hold you accountable to live a
balanced life.

☐ Encourage a friend who is struggling with balance.

☐ Put someone before yourself—find a person with a need and meet
that need.

☐ Begin a journal to keep a record of your challenges and victories.

☐ Take inventory and list the abilities and tools that God has provided
you with.

☐ Memorize Ephesians 6:13—"Take up the whole armor of God, that you
may be able to withstand in the evil day, and having done all,
to stand."

Things to Remember

Everyone who competes for the prize is temperate in all things. Now they do it to obtain a perishable crown, but we for an imperishable crown.

1 CORINTHIANS 9:25 NKJV

Jesus said, "Whoever hears these sayings of Mine, and does them, I will liken him to a wise man who built his house on the rock: and the rain descended, the floods came, and the winds blew and beat on that house; and it did not fall, for it was founded on the rock."

MATTHEW 7:24–25 NKJV

These are evil times, so make every opportunity count.
—Ephesians 5:16 CEV

Giving all diligence, add to your faith virtue; and to virtue knowledge; and to knowledge temperance; and to temperance patience; and to patience godliness; and to godliness brotherly kindness; and to brotherly kindness charity. For if these things be in you, and abound, they make you that ye shall neither be barren nor unfruitful in the knowledge of our Lord Jesus Christ.

2 PETER 1:5–8 KJV

There are six days when you may work, but the seventh day is a Sabbath of rest, a day of sacred assembly. You are not to do any work; wherever you live, it is a Sabbath to the LORD.

LEVITICUS 23:3 NIV

The fruit of the Spirit is love, joy, peace, longsuffering, kindness, goodness, faithfulness, gentleness, self-control. Against such there is no law.

GALATIANS 5:22–23 NKJV

Act like people with good sense and not like fools.

EPHESIANS 5:15 CEV

Let all things be done decently and in order.

1 CORINTHIANS 14:40 NKJV

I am delighted to hear of the careful and orderly ways you conduct your affairs, and impressed with the solid substance of your faith in Christ.

COLOSSIANS 2:5 THE MESSAGE

If we would judge ourselves, we would not be judged.

1 CORINTHIANS 11:31 NKJV

May the God of peace Himself sanctify you completely; and may your whole spirit, soul, and body be preserved blameless at the coming of our Lord Jesus Christ.

1 THESSALONIANS 5:23 NKJV

When first things are put first, second things are not suppressed but increased.
—C. S. LEWIS

Lord, we don't mind who is second as long as Thou art first.
—W. E. STANGTER

Responding to the River's Current

The vessel that he made of clay was marred in the hand of the potter; so he made it again into another vessel, as it seemed good to the potter to make.

—JEREMIAH 18:4 NKJV

A man's world is a world of change. Jobs come and go, relationships and health are unpredictable, and then there's the future—completely unknown. Sometimes change will be your choice and under your direct control; most of the time, however, it won't. But how you respond to change is always your choice.

Imagine yourself riding in a boat down a river. As you go along, you notice that the river changes—again and again and again. It is wide in some parts, narrow in others. There are rapids along some stretches that often give way to areas of calm. In places the water is deep, in others, shallow. The only constant is that the water flows downstream.

Experienced river riders all have their own techniques, but they've learned the basics:

Resistance is futile. You will never be able to change

the course of the river. Success depends on your ability to ride it out, responding quickly and decisively to its twists and turns, ups and downs.

Choose the right type of boat. If you insist on a rowboat, you'll be spending a lot of time in the water. A rowboat isn't designed for a river. It isn't capable of moving with the current.

Bring the right equipment. Without your oars, steering your craft is impossible. And don't forget your life preserver. The best swimmer in the world would have trouble holding his head above water in a stretch of rapids.

Plan on getting wet—because you will. The river will see to that.

The river is a lot like life—your life, any life. It cuts its own unique path through the landscape and carries you along for the ride. Remember these principles as you respond to the changes it brings:

Resistance to the changes in your life is futile. Ask God to help you ride out the twists and turns, responding appropriately to each one.

Don't start down the river of life in the wrong boat. Make sure you are riding securely in a daily relationship with God. It's designed for the white water of life.

It wouldn't be wise to try to navigate the changing river of life without your oars: prayer and the Bible. Salvation—receiving God's forgiveness—is your life preserver.

Change is constant and life is messy—you will get wet. Prepare for it by living a life of integrity.

Change is inevitable. Don't get sucked under by the current—ride smart!

I Will

Decide to be committed to change—it's going to happen anyway.

yes   no

Realize that how I respond to change is always my choice.

yes   no

Look on the positive side of a situation that is out of my control.

yes   no

Remember that God is in control, even if I'm not.

yes   no

Allow God to teach me how to respond and adapt to changes in my life.

yes   no

Be an encouragement to others struggling with change.

yes   no

Things to Do

☐ *Take a canoe trip down a river.*

☐ *For fun, count how many times in one day you are affected by any type of change outside your control.*

☐ *Start a journal to record your thoughts and reactions concerning major changes in your life.*

☐ *Write out a prayer of thanksgiving to God for His control of all things.*

☐ *Find a friend who is experiencing change—then ask specifically how you can help during this time of adjustment.*

☐ *For one day, change your daily routine. Write down your thoughts on how that affected you.*

Things to Remember

Today if you hear God's voice speaking to you, do not harden your hearts against him, as the people of Israel did when they rebelled against him in the desert.

HEBREWS 3:15 TLB

The LORD said, "Do not remember the former things, nor consider the things of old. Behold, I will do a new thing, now it shall spring forth; shall you not know it? I will even make a road in the wilderness and rivers in the desert."

ISAIAH 43:18–19 NKJV

The LORD said, "I will give you a new heart and put a new spirit within you; I will take the heart of stone out of your flesh and give you a heart of flesh."

EZEKIEL 36:26 NKJV

The LORD said, "Behold, the former things have come to pass, and new things I declare; before they spring forth I tell you of them."

ISAIAH 42:9 NKJV

Prepare the way of the LORD; make straight in the desert a highway for our God. Every valley shall be exalted and every mountain and hill brought low; the crooked places shall be made straight and the rough places smooth.

ISAIAH 40:3 NKJV

A bend in the road is not the end of the road, unless you fail to make the turn.

—AUTHOR UNKNOWN

Christians are supposed not merely to endure change, nor even to profit by it, but to cause it.

—HARRY EMERSON FOSDICK

Choices

Eenie, Meenie, Minie, More than Chance

Choose for yourselves this day whom you will serve. . . . As for me and my house, we will serve the LORD.

—JOSHUA 24:15 NKJV

Do you remember the old rhyme: "Eenie, Meenie, Minie, Moe. Catch a tiger by the toe. If he hollers, let him go. Eenie, Meenie, Minie, Moe." Simple rhyme, simple choice. But the choices most of us have to make aren't at all simple.

Many men weigh their options carefully. They make lists of pros and cons, try to anticipate the outcome, then choose accordingly. This is a good beginning. But for those really difficult decisions, it may not be enough. Try asking yourself these two important questions: (1) Will your choice keep you in the center of God's will? and (2) How will your decision affect your life and the lives of others?

Take a moment and picture yourself driving along a large multilaned superhighway. The road seems to go on forever, with no end in sight. As you drive, you see a sign with the name of your destination and an arrow pointing straight ahead. No problem—you're on the right road. Now think of that highway as God's Will Express or the highway to heaven. As long as you resist the urge to speed down one of the exits and onto another highway, you're sure to reach your destination.

The most important question to ask yourself when making a decision, big or small, is whether a certain course of action would take you off the highway to God's will and onto another highway. On another highway you could encounter treacherous driving conditions and many hazards. That road could take you away from God and His good purposes for your life.

Once you've answered that question, you still must ask yourself how each course of action will affect others who are traveling down the highway with you. Would changing lanes cause a pileup or send another driver careening off the road? Is your slow speed obstructing traffic? Is your high speed causing you to miss the sights and sounds of the countryside as you drive along?

This analogy can only be taken so far, but it is useful. It provides a mental picture of how you must consider your options. The trouble is that in real life the highway is not so clearly marked. Sometimes the destination signs are obscured. How do you stay on track when that happens?

The Bible is like a road map. It teaches the principles of right and wrong and explains the consequences of each. Reading the Bible every day will help you see in a general sense where your choices will take you. It will also give you insights and perspective on how your choices will affect those around you. If things still seem foggy, ask a bookstore employee to suggest a good Bible study guide or join a Bible study class at your local church.

The wisdom and counsel of others can also be an important resource. Choose your counselors carefully. Look to see if the evidence of sound judgment is present in their lives. Then ask yourself if their advice lines up with God's Word. Does it leave you with a sense of peace deep down inside?

Don't forget about prayer. Ask God to help you sort through all the incidentals and see His wisdom with clarity. Ask Him to help you cut through your negative mind-sets and biases and give you a clear view of the road ahead. And then listen for His voice inside your heart pointing you to what is right.

Life is filled with decisions—and they seem to just keep coming. But you won't run off the road as long as you set your mind on your destination and keep a close eye on the road signs. Discipline yourself not to act rashly. Take time to give careful consideration to your choices—especially those that will have a lasting effect on your life. Write out the pros and cons. But then do more. Ask yourself those difficult questions, and then search out the answers through Bible study, godly counsel, and prayer.

Free will is an awesome gift. It would have been easy enough for God to make all your choices for you. But He has placed His confidence in you, believing that knowing His will and purpose, you will choose to stay on the road He has set before you.

I Will

Allow God to lead me in my decision making.   _yes_   _no_

Consider how my choices will affect my life and the
lives of others.   _yes_   _no_

Always look to make choices that are in line with
biblical principles.   _yes_   _no_

Be honest with myself about my motivation for
choosing a certain way.   _yes_   _no_

Seek out wise counsel for the weightier decisions in
my life.   _yes_   _no_

Things to Do

☐ Select a rock—large or small—to be placed in your work area as a
reminder to consider the ripple effect of your decisions.

☐ Pray specifically for wisdom before making your next big decision.

☐ Help a family member or friend work through a difficult choice they
have to make.

☐ Find a person who has a history of making wise choices. Go to them
the next time you need advice.

☐ Read about Lot's selfish choice in Genesis 13:5–13. Then read about
how God blessed Abraham in verses 14–17.

☐ The next time you are tempted, write down how you responded. Did
you choose obedience instead of sin?

Things to Remember

I call heaven and earth as witnesses today against you, that I have set before you life and death, blessing and cursing; therefore choose life, that both you and your descendants may live.

DEUTERONOMY 30:19 NKJV

Do not envy the oppressor, and choose none of his ways; for the perverse person is an abomination to the LORD, but His secret counsel is with the upright.

PROVERBS 3:31–32 NKJV

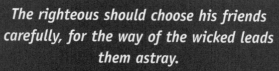

The righteous should choose his friends carefully, for the way of the wicked leads them astray.
—Proverbs 12:26 NKJV

Where there is no counsel, the people fall; but in the multitude of counselors there is safety.

PROVERBS 11:14 NKJV

The entrance of Your words gives light; it gives understanding to the simple.

PSALM 119:130 NKJV

Sound advice is a beacon, good teaching is a light, moral discipline is a life path.

PROVERBS 6:23 THE MESSAGE

Let each of you look out not only for his own interests, but also for the interests of others.

PHILIPPIANS 2:4 NKJV

Whoever listens to me will dwell safely, and will be secure, without fear of evil.

PROVERBS 1:33 NKJV

The way of a fool is right in his own eyes, but he who heeds counsel is wise.

PROVERBS 12:15 NKJV

The counsel of the LORD stands forever, the plans of His heart to all generations.

PSALM 33:11 NKJV

Point me down your highway, GOD; direct me along a well-lighted street.

PSALM 27:11 THE MESSAGE

Remember that those who do good prove that they are God's children.

3 JOHN 1:11 NLT

In a powerful way the word of the Lord kept spreading and growing.

ACTS 19:20 NCV

Every moment you have a choice, regardless of what has happened before. Choose right now to move forward positively and confidently into your incredible future.

—AUTHOR UNKNOWN

Nothing is more difficult, and therefore more precious, than to be able to decide.

—NAPOLEON I. MAXIMS

Creativity

Thinking and Living Outside the Box

My heart is overflowing with a good theme; I recite my composition concerning the King; my tongue is the pen of a ready writer.

—PSALM 45:1 NKJV

You may not think of yourself as a creative person, but you are. You don't have to be an artist, a musician, or an architect to be considered creative. Have you ever stopped to think about a problem and then come up with a solution that was out of the ordinary, and yet was still quite effective? Creativity doesn't have to be extraordinary, but it can be. There are countless situations in everyday life that cause a man to draw on his inner imagination, to think and live outside the box. And whether you realize it or not, you have some of that inside you. God placed it there, and He expects you to use it.

Here is a simple test to illustrate the concept of creative thinking—more specifically, thinking outside the box. By the way, that's a hint! Place three rows of three dots on a sheet of paper. They should look something like this:

Without lifting your pen from the paper, draw four straight lines and connect all of the dots in the image above. Your lines may be vertical, horizontal, or diagonal, and they may cross each other, but you are restricted to using only four straight lines, and your pen must not lift off the paper. Read on when you are ready for the solution.

Thinking outside the box is the key to the solution—literally. Start by drawing a line from the bottom right corner diagonally to the top left. Drop straight down the left side, but continue past the bottom left dot into the open white space. Draw your third line diagonally to the upper right, through the bottom center dot and on through the right side middle dot, again continuing past the boundary of the image until your line stops level with the top row. Your fourth and final line will head left through the entire top row of dots.

Life is full of restrictions and rules. But if you can understand the nature of those restrictions and rules, you can look past them to imagine what is not restricted. That is the beginning of creativity—looking for what could be done, even though it has not been spelled out.

Did you know that God works outside the box? He is our source of creativity—after all, man was created in God's image. During the days of Noah, when mankind was evil in the sight of the Lord, God came up with the idea of using a flood to wipe out all but Noah's family and two of every species of animal. God not only made the lions, but He shut the mouths of the lions when Daniel was thrown into the den with them. God caused the walls of Jericho to fall through an ingenious battle plan that called for marching around the city walls, blowing trumpets, and shouting. Try that today! God even caused a mute donkey to speak so that Balaam would be stopped in his tracks. And God's ultimate outside-the-box idea is His plan of salvation. Who could have thought up that one but God Himself?

There's no arguing that God loves to work outside the box in our lives. If this is true, then ask yourself why you try so hard to conform and fit into the boundaries of boxes everywhere you go. You have been taught to try certain solutions and encouraged to do what has been done before. It's safer and easier. It's inside the box.

Take inventory of yourself for a moment. Think of what you do on a day-to-day basis. Do you make a product or build something out of parts? Do you plan, design, and imagine the possibilities? Are you inventive and productive? Do you like to discover or research? Can you comfort someone and listen? Are you a person who is sensitive to the needs of others? Guess what, you are drawing on the creativity that God has placed inside you.

Where can you think and live creatively in your life—at home, at work, in relationships? Each man's life is different and each man faces different situations. But every man can draw on the same source of creativity—God.

I Will

Accept myself as a creation of God, made in
His image.
      yes   _no_

Appreciate the creativity of others as they
exhibit it in their lives.
      yes   _no_

Consider all options when faced with possible
solutions to a problem.
      yes   _no_

Allow God to use me where and when I least
expect it.
      yes   _no_

Guard myself against going along with the
status quo.
      yes   _no_

Things to Do

☐ *Ask God to show you ways to think and live outside the box.
Make a list.*

☐ *Think of a unique way to tell someone close to you that you love him
or her—then do it.*

☐ *The next time you have a situation that demands creative thought, do
something unusual to stimulate your creativity, such as marching
around the room seven times and shouting.*

☐ *Acknowledge someone else's creativity by recognizing them in front of
their peers.*

☐ *Make a list of some ways God worked outside the box in the stories of
the Bible.*

☐ *Make a list of ways that God has worked outside the box in your life.*

Things to Remember

I will quickly obey your commands, because you have
made me happy.

PSALM 119:32 THE MESSAGE

Make me to know your ways, O Lord; teach me your paths.

PSALM 25:4 THE MESSAGE

Invent your own new song to him; give him a trumpet fanfare.

PSALM 33:3 THE MESSAGE

*I wisdom dwell with prudence, and find out
knowledge of witty inventions.*
—Proverbs 8:12 KJV

Speak to one another with psalms, hymns and spiritual songs.
Sing and make music in your heart to the Lord.

EPHESIANS 5:19 NIV

Just as our bodies have many parts and each part has a special
function, so it is with Christ's body. . . . God has given each of us
the ability to do certain things well.

ROMANS 12:4, 6 NLT

I'll be the poet who sings your glory—
and live what I sing every day.

PSALM 61:8 THE MESSAGE

Let us not become conceited, or irritate
one another, or be jealous of one
another. Dear brothers and sisters, if
another Christian is overcome by some
sin, you who are godly should gently
and humbly help that person back onto
the right path. And be careful not to fall
into the same temptation yourself.

GALATIANS 5:26—6:1 NLT

All must test their own work; then that
work, rather than their neighbor's work,
will become a cause for pride. For all
must carry their own loads.

GALATIANS 6:4–5 NRSV

God can do anything, you know—far
more than you could ever imagine or
guess or request in your wildest dreams!
He does it not by pushing us around but
by working within us, his Spirit deeply
and gently within us.

EPHESIANS 3:20 THE MESSAGE

He hath put a new song in my mouth,
even praise unto our God: many shall
see it, and fear, and shall trust in
the LORD.

PSALM 40:3 KJV

There is a fountain of youth. It is your mind, your talents, the creativity you bring in your life and the lives of people you love.

—SOPHIA LOREN

Creativity has been built into every one of us; it's part of our design. Each of us lives less of the life God intended for us when we choose not to live out the creative powers we possess.

—TED ENGSTROM

Fun

Don't Always Take Life So Seriously

To everything there is a season, a time for every purpose under heaven.

—ECCLESIASTES 3:1 NKJV

A man's responsibilities can take up almost every waking moment. Balancing the demands of a career and oftentimes a family can leave even the strongest man feeling washed out and overwhelmed. But all work and no play can be damaging and counterproductive. Even the busiest man needs to set aside a little time for fun—time to laugh and shrug off your worries, time to relax your muscles and loosen your nerves, time to recover your balance and regain your perspective.

If you're like most men, you may actually feel guilty about having fun when there are still so many things to do. But taking time for play is not, as many believe, a worthless pursuit. Even twenty minutes shooting hoops in the driveway or running your dog on the beach or shooting a round of pool in the rec room at work can help you dump tension, unlock creativity, and rekindle energy.

Would you be surprised to hear that fun can also improve your spiritual life? Did you think that God and fun just don't mix? Consider for a moment that God created your sense of humor right along with your sense of responsibility. He wants you to exercise both. He knows that all fun and no responsibility will leave you feeling empty and hopeless, but all responsibility and no fun will make you brittle, legalistic, and embittered.

Chances are that Jesus had some fun with His disciples. He shared meals with them and traveled with them. It's unlikely that every moment of every day was spent in deep reflection and meditation. They made friends and touched lives along the way.

What types of things do you enjoy doing? What activities do you consider fun? Do you like to play with your kids? Hunt or fish? Swim or workout? Engage in some sport? Take in a movie? Read? Tackle a crossword puzzle? Take a few minutes to think of two activities you would love to engage in if you just had the time. Then make time. You will be shocked to find that a twenty-minute break in the morning can actually facilitate a 5:00 P.M. deadline.

If you are one of those men who take a fun break on a regular basis, feel good about it. Congratulate yourself for being smarter than the average bear. If you aren't taking time to play, it's time to wise up! You'll be better off for it.

I Will

Look for the fun in life.

yes _no_

Resolve to include fun in my daily routines.

yes _no_

Carefully reflect before taking on new
responsibilities.

yes _no_

Try to be more spontaneous.

yes _no_

Recognize that God wants me to live a
balanced life.

yes _no_

Thank God for the ability to enjoy my life.

yes _no_

Encourage another person to take time away from
the daily grind and have some fun.

yes _no_

Things to Do

☐ _Think back to some activity you did that was fun and do it again._

☐ _Make a list of what you consider to be enjoyable things to do._

☐ _Plan to leave work early one day and spend it doing whatever seems
like fun to you._

☐ _Turn your cell phone off for a few hours and don't feel guilty about it!_

☐ _Play a game with your kids, family, or friends._

☐ _Turn a task at your work into a game to make it fun._

☐ _Treat a coworker, family member, or friend to a fun time—coffee,
bowling, movie, sports, golfing, fishing, hunting, driving, whatever you
can both agree on that you both will enjoy._

Things to Remember

It is good and fitting for one to eat and drink, and to enjoy the good of all his labor in which he toils under the sun all the days of his life which God gives him; for it is his heritage.

ECCLESIASTES 5:18 NKJV

Jesus said, "I have come that they may have life, and that they may have it more abundantly."

JOHN 10:10 NKJV

When you win, we plan to raise the roof and lead the parade with our banners. May all your wishes come true!

PSALM 20:5 THE MESSAGE

Celebrate GOD. Sing together—everyone! All you honest hearts, raise the roof!

PSALM 32:11 THE MESSAGE

You'll welcome us with open arms when we run for cover to you. Let the party last all night! Stand guard over our celebration. You are famous, God, for welcoming God-seekers, for decking us out in delight.

PSALM 5:11–12 THE MESSAGE

A good and wholesome thing is a little harmless fun in this world; it tones a body up and keeps him human and prevents him from souring.

—MARK TWAIN

Whence comes this idea that if what we are doing is fun, it can't be God's will: The God who made giraffes, a baby's fingernails, a puppy's tail, a crook necked squash, the bobwhite's call, and a young girl's giggle, has a sense of humor. Make no mistake about that.

—CATHERINE MARSHALL

Health

Regular Maintenance for Your Heart

I pray that you may prosper in all things and be in health, just as your soul prospers.

—3 John 2 NKJV

Tom was one of the fortunate ones. He survived his heart attack at age forty-five. It was 9:15 on a Monday morning when he first experienced a sharp pain between his shoulder blades. The pain then radiated down both of his arms and Tom's breathing grew heavy and labored. He recognized the symptoms quickly and a friend rushed him from work to a nearby hospital for emergency care.

After a year of rehabilitation, a major change of eating and exercise habits, and daily doses of heart medication, Tom is a walking example of a heart-attack survivor. Today he leads a normal life, but he constantly checks himself for symptoms of heart disease. With a little more than 10 percent of his heart having suffered severe damage, Tom is still a risk for future heart problems, especially if he doesn't regularly maintain his heart.

Normally the first symptom of heart trouble for men is

sudden death. And the vast majority of heart attacks for American men happen around 9:00 A.M. on Mondays, just like Tom's. Strange, isn't it? The weekend warrior comes off of a wonderful two-day excursion into fun and frivolity only to arrive at work on Monday with chest pains and a heart that is dying. Men cannot know they have heart disease unless they know some of the major symptoms to look for.

Indicators of potential physical heart attack are elevated high cholesterol, chest pain—angina, weakness—lack of energy, overweight, and lack of exercise.

Mike is one of the unfortunate ones. He suffered a spiritual heart attack—dying without Jesus. At age fifty-two Mike died without knowing Jesus as his Savior. The signs were there, but he ignored the symptoms and continued living life on his own. Mike felt the pain in his chest, an emptiness that only Jesus could fill. He had a friend that had tried to introduce him to the heavenly Physician that could cure Mike's spiritual heart disease, but Mike wanted to treat the symptoms himself—which pretty much meant ignoring them altogether.

Even men who know Jesus can suffer some of the symptoms of spiritual heart disease. Many of the symptoms show up on Sunday mornings. Strange, isn't it? Hard working men come off of a productive week at work, only to find that they have neglected their spiritual health during the week. They arrive at church on Sunday in a spiritual condition that needs immediate attention. Men cannot know they have spiritual heart disease unless they know some of the major symptoms to look for.

Indicators of potential spiritual heart attack are elevated

self importance and independence, chest pain—emptiness, weak prayer life, overemphasis on worldly things, lack of interest in church or Bible study.

It's time to start taking care of your physical heart as well as your spiritual heart. In regard to your physical heart, you should visit a doctor for regular checkups. Take inventory of your heart's health, get your cholesterol checked, and reduce your fat intake. Low-fat meals and tasty recipes are getting easier to find. Increase your exercise routine by taking up a new sport or activity—activity being the key word. If you do not know your target heart rate, check with your doctor first, then hook up with a trainer, even if it's for only one or two visits to get you started on a program. Find a friend who will help hold you accountable as you focus on your heart-healthy habits. There are also health-related books on the topic of maintaining a healthy heart. Check them out and get started taking care of your heart.

Spiritually, you should visit with your heavenly Physician through regular prayer, taking spiritual inventory to determine where your relationship is with God. Increase your fellowship with other Christians. Get involved in a Bible study and find someone you can check in with for accountability. The next time you take the pulse of your physical heartbeat, use that as a reminder to check your spiritual heartbeat. And, wouldn't you know it, there is also a book on the topic of maintaining a healthy spiritual heart—the Bible.

I Will

Strive to spend more time with my heavenly
Physician through prayer checkups.

yes   *no*

Take responsibility for the condition of my physical
and spiritual health.

yes   *no*

Encourage others who are focusing on their own
heart health.

yes   *no*

Remind myself to watch for the symptoms of
spiritual or physical heart disease.

yes   *no*

Determine to make my relationship with Jesus a
priority.

yes   *no*

Things to Do

- [ ] *See your doctor for a physical checkup.*

- [ ] *Begin a regular exercise program.*

- [ ] *Find a friend who is willing to hold you accountable on your exercise program.*

- [ ] *Ask a friend to hold you accountable on your spiritual health.*

- [ ] *Ask God for guidance concerning your next healthy-versus-unhealthy choice.*

- [ ] *Pick a time to physically relax for an hour—and then relax by reading, watching a favorite TV program, or exercising.*

- [ ] *Find out what your target heart rate is so you are able to exercise effectively.*

Things to Remember

Jesus said, "Those who are well have no need of a physician, but those who are sick. I did not come to call the righteous, but sinners, to repentance."

—MARK 2:17 NKJV

He was wounded for our transgressions, He was bruised for our iniquities; the chastisement for our peace was upon Him, and by His stripes we are healed.

ISAIAH 53:5 NKJV

Bless the LORD, O my soul; and all that is within me, bless His holy name! . . . who forgives all your iniquities, who heals all your diseases.
—Psalm 103:1, 3 NKJV

God anointed Jesus of Nazareth with the Holy Spirit and with power, who went about doing good and healing all who were oppressed by the devil, for God was with Him.

ACTS 10:38 NKJV

He himself bore our sins in his body on the tree, so that we might die to sins and live for righteousness; by his wounds you have been healed.

1 PETER 2:24 NIV

O LORD my God, I cried out to You, and You healed me.

PSALM 30:2 NKJV

He sent His word and healed them, and delivered them from their destructions.

PSALM 107:20 NKJV

Do not be wise in your own eyes; fear the LORD and depart from evil. It will be health to your flesh, and strength to your bones.

PROVERBS 3:7–8 NKJV

My son, give attention to my words; incline your ear to my sayings. Do not let them depart from your eyes; keep them in the midst of your heart; for they are life to those who find them, and health to all their flesh.

PROVERBS 4:20–22 NKJV

If we would judge ourselves, we would not be judged. But when we are judged, we are chastened by the Lord, that we may not be condemned with the world.

1 CORINTHIANS 11:31–32 NKJV

Pleasant words are like a honeycomb, sweetness to the soul and health to the bones.

PROVERBS 16:24 NKJV

To be "whole" is to be spiritually, emotionally, and physically healthy. Jesus lived in perfect wholeness.

—COLIN URQUHART

Look to your health; and if you have it, praise God, and value it next to a good conscience; for health is the second blessing that we mortals are capable of; a blessing that money cannot buy.

—IZAAK WALTON

Family Traditions

More than Turkey Dinners and Mistletoe

Tell it to your children, and let your children tell it to their children, and their children to the next generation.

JOEL 1:3 NIV

When Christmas rolls around this year and you are searching the malls or surfing the Internet for presents for your family, don't forget to consider one of the greatest gifts you could ever give: tradition. Just as God gave His Word as a reminder of your spiritual heritage with Him, He wants you to pass along enriching stories and important values to your family.

Have you given much thought to your traditions— how they started or what has made them endure over generations? Who carves the turkey each Thanksgiving? Or does your family serve something else? Do you watch parades or just football? Why do family members take a walk after that special November dinner but not after dinner on any other day? Whose house do you go to on Christmas? Do you celebrate and open gifts on Christmas Eve or Christmas day? When do you put up the Christmas tree? Is it artificial or fresh-cut? What is a no-no when it comes to decorating it?

On the surface these traditions don't seem that significant. But they are. Each one is important to who you are and what has shaped your family. Each tradition is one more bond that connects your past with your family's future as your children and grandchildren to come follow the same traditions.

How do you keep traditions or begin new ones? By talking together as a family about what you like best about traditional things you do during the holidays. You and your wife may have done things differently in your families of origin, but think of how you can pick out the best from both your rituals to create one that your kids can claim as their own. You and your wife still hold on to your own versions while making something unique for your family.

The Bible is full of traditions. In fact, since they didn't have history books back then, it was the retelling of family stories and keeping of their religious holiday traditions that kept them mindful of their heritage and God's promises. God wanted His people to remember the Passover as a testament to His saving grace. He wants Christians to take Communion to remember what Jesus did for us on the cross.

Pray about your family traditions. Ask God to fill you and your wife with creativity as you think of ways to establish new customs. And thank Him for your family and the special ways He has given you to celebrate and remember holiday seasons.

I Will

Think of cherished childhood traditions that I can
pass along to my family.   yes   no

Blend new and old traditions during the holidays.   yes   no

Be open to suggestions from my wife and kids about
changes they'd like to see in my traditions.   yes   no

Make sure faith in God is a big part of our
family story.   yes   no

Involve extended family in some traditions.   yes   no

Focus more on my family than on the tradition itself.   yes   no

Stay calm and collected and learn to cope if a
tradition doesn't happen one year.   yes   no

Things to Do

☐ *Make a list of major holidays and decide as a family where and how
you will spend them.*

☐ *Fold in your and your wife's family traditions to the new ones being
created by you and your children.*

☐ *Put together a book for each of your children with family pictures,
stories, and recipes for them to remember and pass on to their
children.*

☐ *Take a family Christmas photo at the same place each year, sitting or
standing in the same positions.*

☐ *For Thanksgiving, let each family member be responsible for one menu
item to prepare annually.*

Things to Remember

You must continue in the things which you have learned and been assured of, knowing from whom you have learned them.

2 TIMOTHY 3:14 NKJV

Listen to me, you who pursue righteousness, who seek the LORD: Look to the rock from which you were hewn and to the quarry from which you were dug.

ISAIAH 51:1 NASB

Children's children are a crown to the aged, and parents are the pride of their children.

PROVERBS 10:6 NIV

According to the grace of God which was given to me, as a wise master builder I have laid the foundation, and another builds on it. But let each one take heed how he builds on it.

1 CORINTHIANS 3:10 NCV

We have heard with our ears, O God, our fathers have told us, the deeds You did in their days, in days of old.

PSALM 44:1 NKJV

My family history begins with me, but yours ends with you.

—PLATO

Up at the folks' house, Christmas is the exact same as it's been forever. You close your eyes and it could be any time. You might open them and you'd be six years old, not forty-two.

—GARRISON KEILLOR

Humor and Laughter

Medicine that Doesn't Come from a Pharmacy

A time to weep, and a time to laugh; a time to mourn, and a time to dance.

—ECCLESIASTES 3:4 NKJV

Did you know that the ability to laugh is a gift from God? That's right. God has seen fit to create humans with a unique appreciation of humor and all things funny. He has made it a basic characteristic of all humankind—though creative and unique in its expression.

In fact, the ability to laugh and see humor in the circumstances of our lives plays an important role in our mental well-being. It works as a safety valve, providing needed relief from the pressures that build up inside.

If you are a typical man, you undoubtedly have your share of deadlines, work responsibilities, financial stress, personal obligations, and more. Then there are the pressures you place on yourself, like career expectations, and personal goals. Humor and laughter help you push out what has built up inside.

Think of it this way: If you blow air into a balloon, it

expands. Keep adding air pressure, and the balloon will become full. Continue, and the balloon will eventually weaken and break. When you laugh, it's like letting some of the air out of the balloon before it becomes full enough to burst. Don't let pressure steal your joy. Smile for a moment. Whoosh!

The sweet release of laughter is important to your physical health as well. The list of stress-related illnesses gets longer every day, including such monsters as heart disease and arthritis. Stress weakens your immune system and makes you more vulnerable to everything from the common cold to cancer.

If you find yourself filling with pressure like a balloon about to burst, laugh. Think of it as your God-given right and your personal responsibility. Laughter is your safety valve. If you just can't find anything funny about your own life right now, take in a funny movie or watch a TV show, read a humorous book, ask if anyone has heard a good joke lately. Listen to your children's conversations. Watch your dog or cat at play. Observe life and learn to see humor in everyday things. God can show you humor in the least likely places.

God doesn't want you to be uptight and about to burst. He wants you to live a life filled with joy—even during the difficult times in your life. So bring in the clowns and let the healing release of laughter flow.

I Will

Maintain my emotional health with humor and laughter.

yes   *no*

Allow God to show me humor in everyday situations.

yes   *no*

Try to relax when life's pressures begin to build.

yes   *no*

Start taking myself less seriously.

yes   *no*

Accept myself as a creation of God, made in His image.

yes   *no*

Exhibit joy in my life.

yes   *no*

Remind others that they need to take their laughter "medicine."

yes   *no*

Things to Do

☐ *Hang a deflated balloon in a prominent place as a reminder to laugh.*

☐ *Practice smiling in a mirror.*

☐ *Read a humorous story or the Sunday comics.*

☐ *Choose one thing about yourself that you can start taking less seriously.*

☐ *Spend a half-hour noticing the humor in life around you.*

☐ *Read Proverbs 17:22 every morning for one week.*

☐ *Learn a joke that can be shared with a friend the next time he or she needs a good laugh.*

Things to Remember

A merry heart does good, like medicine, but a broken spirit dries the bones.

PROVERBS 17:22 NKJV

He who is of a merry heart has a continual feast.

PROVERBS 15:15 NKJV

Those who went off with heavy hearts will come home laughing, with armloads of blessing.

PSALM 126:6 THE MESSAGE

I will be glad and rejoice in Your mercy, for You have considered my trouble; You have known my soul in adversities.

PSALM 31:7 NKJV

On your feet now—applaud GOD! Bring a gift of laughter, sing yourselves into his presence.

PSALM 100:1 THE MESSAGE

I'm whistling, laughing, and jumping for joy; I'm singing your song, High God.

PSALM 9:2 THE MESSAGE

Always laugh when you can; it is cheap medicine.
Merriment is a philosophy not well understood. It is the sunny side of existence.

—LORD BYRON

Laughter can relieve tension, soothe the pain of disappointment, and strengthen the spirit for the formidable tasks that always lie ahead.

—DWIGHT D. EISENHOWER

Joy

A Smile that Starts in Your Heart

In Your presence is fullness of joy.

—PSALM 16:11 NKJV

Happiness, you know; joy, you're maybe not so clear. Most men don't think of joy as a very manly concept. When your team won the Super Bowl, did you jump up and down, proclaiming that you were filled with joy? Probably not!

Joy is a special kind of happiness. It describes an emotion that rises up from within and is more closely associated with spirit and soul than with mind and body. You may be happy one day and unhappy the next, but your sense of joy stays constant throughout. This is true because happiness is based on the circumstances that change, but joy is based on those circumstances that don't change.

When the angels announced the birth of Jesus to the shepherds watching their flocks of sheep in the fields, they did not say, "We have good news that's going to make you real happy." Instead, an angel of the Lord announced, "I bring you good tidings of great joy." God wasn't announcing the birth of a king who would sit on an earthly throne for a certain number of years, improving the lives of his subjects. He was announcing the birth of the King of kings, His very own Son, the permanent and unchanging solution to the problem of sin.

In the midst of terrible persecution, James wrote to the early Christians. He urged them to approach their suffering with a sense of joy, knowing that their trials were producing lasting character in their lives.

Do you have a sense of joy deep inside? A sense of delight that is unaffected by your outward circumstances?

God wants you to know that when you enter into a relationship with Him, He will fill your heart with joy—the joy that comes from knowing that you are eternally secure in the arms of your heavenly Father. No matter what you face in life, that joy will flow up from deep within, nourishing and sustaining you.

Open your heart to God today. Ask Him to come in and stay forever and ever, through thick and thin, good and bad. He's knocking on your door right now.

You may have experienced the joy that comes from knowing Jesus, but sense that it is no longer flowing freely from within. It could be that you have turned your eyes from those things that are certain and lasting to those things that are temporary and fleeting. Turn your eyes back to God and ask Him to help you feel the joy of your salvation once again.

I Will

Recognize the difference between joy
and happiness.

<u>*yes*</u>   <u>*no*</u>

Determine to take hold of the joy of the Lord.

<u>*yes*</u>   <u>*no*</u>

Remind myself often that the joy of the Lord is not
subject to my circumstances.

<u>*yes*</u>   <u>*no*</u>

Release my inner joy by focusing on those things
that are permanent and lasting.

<u>*yes*</u>   <u>*no*</u>

Let the joy of the Lord comfort me especially in the
midst of difficult circumstances.

<u>*yes*</u>   <u>*no*</u>

Determine to allow the joy of the Lord to flow
through me to others.

<u>*yes*</u>   <u>*no*</u>

Things to Do

☐ *Make a list of the good things in my life that will not change.*

☐ *Write down my thoughts concerning the difference between happiness and joy.*

☐ *Compose a joyful poem or song to the Lord, describing my respect and admiration.*

☐ *Memorize James 1:2–3—"My brethren, count it all joy when you fall into various trials, knowing that the testing of your faith produces patience."*

☐ *Make a list of friends and family members who don't seem to be experiencing God's joy in their lives. Commit to pray specifically for them each day for a month.*

Things to Remember

With joy you will draw water from the wells of salvation.

ISAIAH 12:3 NKJV

Do not sorrow, for the joy of the LORD is your strength.

NEHEMIAH 8:10 NKJV

Though you have not seen him, you love him; and even though you do not see him now, you believe in him and are filled with an inexpressible and glorious joy, for you are receiving the goal of your faith, the salvation of your souls.

1 PETER 1:8–9 NIV

My soul shall be joyful in the LORD; it shall rejoice in His salvation.

PSALM 35:9 NKJV

Why are you cast down, O my soul? And why are you disquieted within me? Hope in God, for I shall yet praise Him for the help of His countenance.

PSALM 42:5 NKJV

A cheerful heart brings a smile to your face; a sad heart makes it hard to get through the day.

PROVERBS 15:13 THE MESSAGE

Happiness depends on what happens; joy does not. Remember, Jesus Christ had joy, and He prays, "that they might have my joy fulfilled in themselves."

—OSWALD CHAMBERS

Joy is the experience of knowing that you are unconditionally loved.

—HENRI NOUWEN

Learning

Expanding the Mind

Give instruction to a wise man, and he will be still wiser; teach a just man, and he will increase in learning.

Some people dislike school and some can't get enough of it. Interestingly, both of these groups include intelligent, inquisitive people. No matter which group you fall into, it's wise to keep your mind open to new things and your brain tuned to discovery mode.

Nick knew he should sign up for the computer class being offered at work, but he held back. Although he knew he was already behind in terms of his computer skills, he just couldn't make himself commit to six weeks of classes. *I'm not exactly computer illiterate*, he told himself. I know enough to get along.

But he soon realized that his coworkers were putting together charts and spreadsheets, while he struggled even with the simple tasks. When the second class came along, Nick put his reluctance and fears behind him. Soon he was marveling at the time and effort saved by his new skills. And when it was time for his review, completing the class earned him a raise.

Are you one of those people who shrink back from learning new things? If so, you may find yourself at the back of the pack. Carving a new track in your brain can be an intimidating prospect, but it is rarely a useless endeavor. These suggestions may help:

Start at the beginning. If you find that you need instruction in a certain area, don't hesitate to take a basic course first that will familiarize you with concepts and terminology. Doing so doesn't mean you're dumb—it means you're smart!

Explore all your options. If you don't do well in a classroom situation, find someone who can tutor you on a person-to-person basis.

Take it slow. If you haven't been challenged to learn something new for awhile, it may take some time to get those neurons firing again. Hang in there. It will get easier as you go along.

Don't give up. The biggest mistake you can make is to panic and quit. It's possible to be clueless one minute and have a flash of understanding the next. Even geniuses experience that.

It's also important to keep your mind fresh and growing in regard to godly character and your relationship with God. As you read your Bible, ask God to open your mind to new insights concerning your Christian experience.

Learning is important at every age in all areas of life. Determine that you will be a wise man open to instruction.

I Will

Acknowledge the benefits of lifelong learning.   *yes*   *no*

Confess my fear of learning new things.   *yes*   *no*

Surrender my biases about learning to God.   *yes*   *no*

Determine to be courageous in my encounters
with learning.   *yes*   *no*

Deal with the pride that keeps me from admitting
there is something I don't know.   *yes*   *no*

Ask God to give me a hunger for spiritual
understanding.   *yes*   *no*

Be thankful for a sound mind.   *yes*   *no*

Things to Do

☐ *Make a list of the areas where you need to improve your skills with increased knowledge.*

☐ *Write down your thoughts about the learning process and how it affects you.*

☐ *Pick up a course catalog from the nearest community college and use it to look into the areas in which you need further education.*

☐ *Memorize two scriptures on the subject of learning: Proverbs 9:9— "Give instruction to a wise man, and he will be still wiser; teach a just man, and he will increase in learning"; 2 Timothy 2:15—"Be diligent to present yourself approved to God, a worker who does not need to be ashamed, rightly dividing the word of truth."*

☐ *Find one of those people who love school and ask him or her to give you some tips on study techniques. Write them down for future use.*

Things to Remember

When wisdom enters your heart, and knowledge is pleasant to your soul, discretion will preserve you; understanding will keep you.

PROVERBS 2:10–11 NKJV

A scoffer seeks wisdom and does not find it, but knowledge is easy to him who understands.

PROVERBS 14:6 NKJV

A wise man will hear and increase learning, and a man of understanding will attain wise counsel.

PROVERBS 1:5 NKJV

Learn to do good; seek justice, rebuke the oppressor; defend the fatherless, plead for the widow.

ISAIAH 1:17 NKJV

Study to show thyself approved unto God, a workman that needeth not to be ashamed, rightly dividing the word of truth.

2 TIMOTHY 2:15 KJV

Whatever things were written before were written for our learning, that we through the patience and comfort of the Scriptures might have hope.

ROMANS 15:4 NKJV

Anyone who stops learning is old, whether twenty or eighty. Anyone who keeps learning stays young. The greatest thing in life is to keep your mind young.

—HENRY FORD

One's mind is like a knife. If you don't sharpen it, it gets rusty.

—NIEN CHENG

Letting Go

Don't Be a Front-Seat Driver

The LORD said, "I will bring the blind by a way they did not know; I will lead them in paths they have not known. I will make darkness light before them, and crooked places straight. These things I will do for them, and not forsake them."

—ISAIAH 42:16 NKJV

A Christian man pictured his life as being like riding a tandem bicycle with Jesus. He saw himself sitting up front and steering, with Jesus riding on the backseat, always with him. It was comforting for the man to know that Jesus was behind him pedaling, ready to handle any emergencies.

Then one day, Jesus asked the man a question. "Will you trade places with Me?" But the man was not ready to give up the front seat. After all, things seemed to be going along rather nicely. So the man said, "Not today," and they pedaled on together. They continued down familiar roads, passing the same landmarks again and again. Occasionally the man took a wrong turn and got lost and Jesus would quietly point and guide the man back to the right road.

No matter where they went, Jesus was always there, pedaling from the backseat.

Some time passed and again Jesus asked the man, "Will you trade places with Me?" This time the man decided to give up his seat. As Jesus took hold of the handlebars, He looked back at the man, smiled, and said, "Trust Me. Now pedal."

The man discovered immediately that Jesus was taking a different route. When he asked Jesus about it, He replied, "I can take you places that you never knew existed. I know roads that you have never ridden on. I know the paths that lead up mountains and through valleys and along the seashores. I know your abilities, your strengths, and your needs. I can lead you to places where you will make a difference for My kingdom. All you have to do is trust Me to steer while you pedal." So the man pedaled.

The pedaling was strenuous at times, and at others, they seemed to coast along effortlessly. Occasionally the man would offer suggestions to Jesus about what direction they should go next. But Jesus would smile and respond with the words, "Trust Me and pedal." The man allowed Jesus to permanently have the front seat; his life was never again the same.

Where are you in your life? Are you riding a tandem bicycle with Jesus? If not, now is a good time to start. If you already have a relationship with Jesus, are you riding up front? Or have you chosen to let go of the handlebars, take the backseat, and allow Him to steer? Remember—when Jesus is in the front seat, all you need to do is trust Him and pedal!

I Will

Trust God to guide me and I will follow. *yes* *no*

Remind myself that God knows the way. *yes* *no*

Be careful of situations where I am tempted to give God advice or directions. *yes* *no*

Encourage others as they struggle with letting go. *yes* *no*

Stay grounded in my personal relationship with Jesus. *yes* *no*

Identify those areas of my life where I tend to keep control. *yes* *no*

Relinquish control of those areas I have identified to God. *yes* *no*

Things to Do

☐ The next time you sit behind the steering wheel of your vehicle, let it remind you to ask God for guidance.

☐ Read Matthew 4:18–22 and John 1:35–49, the accounts of when Jesus called His disciples.

☐ Ask God to help you resist the urge to call the shots.

☐ Find someone trustworthy who will hold you accountable to live a God-lead life.

☐ Make a list of some areas of your life where you would like to relinquish control to God.

☐ Pray and thank God for His unconditional love for you.

Things to Remember

Jesus said, "Whoever desires to save his life will lose it, but whoever loses his life for My sake will find it."

MATTHEW 16:25 NKJV

Jesus said, "Whoever desires to come after Me, let him deny himself, and take up his cross, and follow Me. For whoever desires to save his life will lose it, but whoever loses his life for My sake and the gospel's will save it."

MARK 8:34–35 NKJV

Jesus answered and said, "Assuredly, I say to you, there is no one who has left house or brothers or sisters or father or mother or wife or children or lands, for My sake and the gospel's, who shall not receive a hundredfold now in this time—houses and brothers and sisters and mothers and children and lands, with persecutions—and in the age to come, eternal life."

MARK 10:29–30 NKJV

Humble yourselves in the sight of the Lord, and He will lift you up.

JAMES 4:10 NKJV

He must increase, but I must decrease.

JOHN 3:29 NKJV

Our satisfaction lies in submission to the divine embrace.

—JAN VAN RUYSBROECK

Carry the cross patiently and with perfect submission and in the end it shall carry you.

—THOMAS À KEMPIS

Nature

Go Take a Hike

Let the field be joyful, and all that is in it.
Then all the trees of the woods will rejoice before the Lord.

—PSALM 96:12 NKJV

When was the last time you spent some quality time outdoors? Have you gone exploring lately? Are you regularly enjoying God in His creation? He was pleased with His masterpiece after He put it together, and He wants you to delight in it too. Most adults, though, look out their back door and only see what needs to be mowed, raked, or shoveled. Children, though, can take a corner of a yard and all of a sudden become Lewis and Clark exploring the West for the first time.

Consider Ecclesiastes 1:9, which says that there is nothing new under the sun. When you first read that, you probably thought about it for a brief second or two, said "Huh," and went on with your life. And as you got older, maybe without even realizing it, your entire outlook on life began to reflect more and more that verse. Nothing new. Life goes on.

But is that how you want to live? Sure, you could base your life on that statement from Solomon. But wouldn't you rather live it knowing that no matter how long you live, no matter how many things you see or how many times you travel around the world, you'll always be able to see something that is new to you? One afternoon this week or next, get out in nature and discover (or rediscover) God's creation. Go to a walking trail or a state park and just take a hike. You'll be surprised by what you find.

For one, you'll feel better physically: fresh air, muscles you had long forgotten, blood and adrenaline pumping through your body. You might feel worn out at the end of your trek, but it won't be that exhausted feeling you get after a ten-hour day at the office.

Second, you'll be able to clear your mind from everything that is pressing on you. Leave your phone and pager at home—along with your mental or written list of chores to be done—and listen to the sounds of nature and for God to speak to your heart.

Finally, you'll quickly find yourself giving praise to God for all His creation. Your eyes will be opened to the littlest wonders you've always taken for granted—the intricacy of a leaf or the hidden lives of bugs under rocks. These are all incredible snapshots of God's love poured out for you. Take this time to reconnect with God and to thank Him for all He has done for you.

I Will

See my backyard as more than something to mow. _yes_ _no_

Think of the world from the perspective of a
little boy. _yes_ _no_

Remember that God created everything big   and
small. _yes_ _no_

Consider one or more of my childhood outdoor
memories. _yes_ _no_

Thank God for letting me be a part of His beautiful
creation. _yes_ _no_

Expect to be wowed when I go on my next
nature hike. _yes_ _no_

Things to Do

☐ *Find something new in your backyard.*

☐ *Give specific praise to God for what you see.*

☐ *Buy a map of a state park and plan out your next trek.*

☐ *Instead of eating at your desk, take your lunch outside.*

☐ *Catch a bug.*

☐ *Buy or create a journal (field notes, if you will) to record your outdoor
experiences and the messages God speaks to your heart.*

☐ *Bring a camera to record what you see.*

Things to Remember

The God of gods, the LORD, speaks. He calls the earth from the rising to the setting sun. God shines from Jerusalem, whose beauty is perfect.

PSALM 50:1–2 NCV

Jesus said, "Consider the lilies, how they grow: they neither toil nor spin; and yet I say to you, even Solomon in all his glory was not arrayed like one of these."

LUKE 12:27 NKJV

Out of the ground the LORD God made every tree grow that is pleasant to the sight and good for food. The tree of life was also in the midst of the garden, and the tree of the knowledge of good and evil.

GENESIS 2:9 NKJV

Solomon's wisdom excelled the wisdom of all the men of the East and all the wisdom of Egypt. . . . Also he spoke of trees, from the cedar tree of Lebanon even to the hyssop that springs out of the wall; he spoke also of animals, of birds, of creeping things, and of fish.

1 KINGS 4:30, 33 NKJV

Nature inanimate employs sweet sounds, But animated nature sweeter still, To soothe and satisfy the human ear.

WILLIAM COWPER

Nature paints the best part of the picture, carves the best of the statue, builds the best part of the house, and speaks the best part of the oration.

—RALPH WALDO EMERSON

Anger

Listen to the Silence

Don't sin by letting anger gain control over you. Think about it overnight and remain silent.

—PSALM 4:4 NLT

Ever get angry? Has a coworker, close friend, or family member ever done something to make you lose your cool? The typical man likes to think that his feathers are not easily ruffled, but most men have a breaking point. When you are angered, you perhaps respond in one of three ways: (1) You strike back immediately and move on; (2) you hold back your feelings and move on; or (3) you don't get angry until you are wronged again—and then you go back to option 1. It's a simple plan that works most of the time. But is it right?

Now consider whether your three typical options actually work for you—and whether they have limited value. When you last got angry and you erupted in anger, did you rid yourself of your negative feelings? If instead you held in your anger, did that work any better?

The Bible has much to say about anger and how to—and how not to—handle it. One way is to deal with it right away, to not let the sun go down on your anger, as the apostle Paul suggested. Another way the Bible says you can handle your anger is to think about a situation overnight and remain silent. So how do you know when you should remain silent—especially when you want to take action right away? You first must assess the situation.

What if someone at work takes all the credit for a project you slaved over for weeks? You probably should wait, pray for guidance, and listen to God for what you should do. He might tell you that everything will be OK in the long run, that you will be rewarded in the future for your accomplishments. In that circumstance, a quick response might be detrimental to your career.

What should you do, though, if someone verbally attacks you in a meeting or publicly denigrates your work for no apparent reason? Then it is probably best not to remain silent for too long. Still, you want to be quiet and ask God to reveal to you what you should say and when you should say it. By remaining quiet and listening for His guidance, you will know that your response will be the right one.

We know that it's OK for us to show anger. Even Jesus showed anger. The not-sinning part is what He had down, though, and what you need to work on. Ask God to fill you with His love and to give you patience as you wait on His answer. By reading God's Word and listening for His counsel, you can learn to respond appropriately.

I Will

Remain patient while seeking God's guidance when I'm angered.

yes   *no*

Remember that being angry is not bad in itself.

yes   *no*

Focus on positive things to put matters in perspective.

yes   *no*

Make time to wait on God.

yes   *no*

Remember my integrity in the face of anger.

yes   *no*

Maintain control of my emotions.

yes   *no*

Be willing to forgive.

yes   *no*

Things to Do

☐ *Write out on paper the different ways you could respond to a situation, and read them aloud before you choose one.*

☐ *Take a walk around the block before saying anything.*

☐ *Write a letter to the person who angered you, read it and reword it if you need to, throw it away and go talk to him or her.*

☐ *Watch a funny sitcom or listen to a comedy CD.*

☐ *Talk to a friend to see how he perceives the situation.*

☐ *If someone in your church has wronged you, get your pastor or a church leader to accompany you when you confront the person.*

☐ *Pray for soft hearts on both sides and an opportunity to seek and accept forgiveness.*

Things to Remember

A soft answer turns away wrath, but a harsh word stirs up anger.

PROVERBS 15:1 NKJV

He who is slow to anger is better than the mighty, and he who rules his spirit than he who takes a city.

PROVERBS 16:32 NKJV

My friends, do not try to punish others when they wrong you, but wait for God to punish them with his anger. It is written: "I will punish those who do wrong; I will repay them," says the LORD.

ROMANS 12:19 NCV

Love is patient, love is kind. It does not envy, it does not boast, it is not proud. It is not rude, it is not self-seeking, it is not easily angered, it keeps no record of wrongs.

1 CORINTHIANS 13:4–5 NIV

Jonathan arose from the table in fierce anger, and ate no food the second day of the month, for he was grieved for David, because his father had treated him shamefully.

1 SAMUEL 20:34 NKJV

Anger is a brief lunacy.

—HORACE

Anger can be cured by time; but hatred cannot. The one aims at giving pain to its object, the other at doing him harm.

—ARISTOTLE

Simplicity

Keeping It Simple

And Jesus said: "I tell you the truth, unless you change and become like little children, you will never enter the kingdom of heaven."

—MATTHEW 18:3 NIV

Do you ever feel overwhelmed because life has become too cluttered or too complex? Maybe you are being pulled in so many directions that you suffer from what could be described as emotional and spiritual vertigo. Or perhaps you are overcommitted to a certain activity for which you are less than enthusiastic. Whatever you are struggling with, it probably all boils down to a lack of simplicity in life. God wants you to live a simple life, because you can then better focus on Him and more easily see how He can use you.

Children need no help with keeping things simple. Often toddlers, when they receive a Christmas or birthday present, find less enjoyment from the gift they receive than from the box in which it came. A seven-year-old boy will spend an hour watching a spider spin its web. A junior-higher will take a skateboard—just a piece of wood and four wheels—and be set for the afternoon.

Adults sometime look at kids and think that they waste their time on trivial things. On the contrary, they are doing what comes naturally to them—enjoying life while keeping things simple. And that is what God wants us to do.

Are there things in your life—physical, spiritual, or emotional—that you need to clear out to make room for more of Jesus? Are any of your material possessions taking the number-one spot in your life and robbing you of your joy? If so, you may have to get rid of them before you are able to move ahead. Or do you have so much stuff in and around your home that time to read, pray, serve others, or enjoy a hobby is never available? Everything you have and do may be good, but it is true that you can get too much of a good thing—especially if good things are keeping you from that which is better.

Jesus promised that if you seek Him first, then all the other things in this life will be added later. That is very simple, something that should be easily accomplished. Only one thing to focus on—your relationship with God—and He will handle all the other pieces of your life. Give it a try. Simplify, and see if your life doesn't end up reflecting this formula: Less equals more.

I Will

Desire to live day by day.   _yes_   _no_

Choose to celebrate the little things.   _yes_   _no_

Remember that God provides for all my needs.   _yes_   _no_

Keep in mind that money cannot buy happiness.   _yes_   _no_

Seek out the contentment that is ready to be
found.   _yes_   _no_

Look at the big picture and strive to live within it.   _yes_   _no_

Take notice of the activities that bring me life and
those that wear me down.   _yes_   _no_

Things to Do

☐ *Make one day a week TV-free.*

☐ *Read a book.*

☐ *Write a letter, stick it in an envelope, put a stamp on it, walk it to your mailbox, and send it off the way you used to do—instead of sending a quick e-mail message.*

☐ *Write out all the things that demand your time and ask God to show which ones are important and which ones aren't.*

☐ *Fill a box up with some possessions you no longer need and donate them to some organization or family.*

☐ *For your devotional time, meditate on and memorize one verse this week—that's all.*

Things to Remember

Our motive for writing is simply this:
We want you to enjoy this too. Your joy
will double our joy!

1 JOHN 1:4 THE MESSAGE

One thing I have desired of the Lord,
that will I seek: that I may dwell in the
house of the Lord all the days of my life,
to behold the beauty of the Lord, and to
inquire in His temple.

PSALM 27:4 NKJV

Continuing daily with one accord in the
temple, and breaking bread from house
to house, they ate their food with
gladness and simplicity of heart.

ACTS 2:46 NKJV

In that hour Jesus rejoiced in the Spirit
and said, "I thank You, Father, Lord of
heaven and earth, that You have hidden
these things from the wise and prudent
and revealed them to babes. Even so,
Father, for so it seemed good in Your
sight."

LUKE 10:21 NKJV

Lord, my heart is not haughty, nor my
eyes lofty. Neither do I concern myself
with great matters, nor with things too
profound for me.

PSALM 131:1 NKJV

Simplicity,
simplicity,
simplicity! I say,
let your affairs be
as two or three,
and not a hundred
or a thousand;
instead of a million
count half a dozen,
and keep your
accounts on your
thumb-nail.

—HENRY DAVID THOREAU

Oh, for the simple
life, for tents and
starry skies!

—ISRAEL ZANGWILL

Other Books in the Checklist for Life Series

Checklist for Life
ISBN 0-7852-6455-8

Checklist for Life for Women
ISBN 0-7852-6462-0

Checklist for Life for Teens
ISBN 0-7852-6461-2